JOY
Unleashed

JOY
Unleashed

The Story of Bella, the Unlikely Therapy Dog

JEAN BAUR

FOREWORD BY AIMÉE SCOTT

Skyhorse Publishing

Memoirs, by definition, are written depictions of events in people's lives. They are memories. All the events in this story are as accurate and truthful as possible. Many names and places have been changed to protect the privacy of others. Mistakes, if any, are caused solely by the passage of time.

CONTENTS

To Beverly and all the wonderful people Bella and I have met in our work as a therapy dog team. And for my five grandchildren: Molly, William, Lucy, Elliott, and Aidan.

FOREWORD

Aimée Scott, Special Education Teacher
December 2015
Stonington, Connecticut

Being a special education teacher is a privilege filled with challenges. These challenges go far beyond teaching reading and math to students who have difficulty learning in the same way or at the same level as their peers. Helping special needs children requires trust, time, and an open mind. It means trying to make decisions that are best for the child, no matter how difficult this makes the teacher's work. And underneath it all is an unconditional commitment to make learning and life better for each child.

When I was first approached about having a therapy dog come to work with my students on a weekly basis, I couldn't have been happier. As a dog lover myself, I knew firsthand how special dogs are and how effective they are at breaking through barriers. I was determined to get through the "red tape" at school to make sure this would be something I could offer my students. With the help of my administrators, Jean and I were able to set up a program with Bella and my students in my first year at a new school.

I admit, I was nervous at first. I had several students who were afraid of dogs, as well as others who had never been near one. Would their parents consent? What would Bella really do with these children? Would she fit in with our curriculum or only be a distraction?

We are now completing two and a half years of having Bella and Jean come to our class each week. Students cuddle up with Jean and read Bella stories on the big cushions. They tell Bella about their day and get her water and treats. They often walk her down the school hallway, a huge status symbol, as the other students can't distract Bella while she's working. She has become a part of our special education resources and a high point for our students. I can't tell you how many times I'm asked each week, "Is it Friday yet?"—the children know that's the day Bella comes to school.

So what difference does it make having a therapy dog in our program? Bella accepts the children exactly as they are. If they can't talk, she doesn't care. If they're struggling to read, she has no judgment. If they were afraid of her, they aren't any longer, as her sweetness has won them over. What I see is that Bella helps build our students' confidence because she wants to be with them. She licks their faces, listens to their stories, plays whatever games they want, and makes them happy. It's always special to be with Bella.

Bella and Jean have changed my program in the best possible way. Their presence has given my students a way to show what they do know, rather than what they don't know. It has reaffirmed that they are wonderful just as they are, and I love seeing their hands stroking Bella's soft, white fur as they read to her. Bella is also fun—she loves rolling on the floor, fetching her ball, prancing down the hallways. I know when Bella visits I will observe the powerful ways this dog reassures the children.

I cannot thank Bella and Jean enough for the changes I see in my students due to their weekly visits. I look forward to the years to come with Bella and Jean, and all the students they will be helping in the future. I hope that more classrooms will be able to have this experience.

INTRODUCTION

Bella, my therapy dog, and I have been visiting The Starfish Home—a rehab facility—for four years (in addition to our work in two hospitals and an elementary school, and a few other places), and one of the residents we visited there was named Rose. She wasn't one of Bella's favorites, as she couldn't talk and didn't give her treats. She was Portuguese and had beautiful posture. She'd sit upright as though entertaining a dignitary, and her eyes brightened when she saw Bella. Her sister was often there in the room, visiting. She thanked me once and said what a relief it was to have a dog in the room—"Just something alive and happy" is how she put it. I nodded and moved Bella as close to Rose as I could, luring her with a treat. Later, I told Rose we would see her the following week, and she waved. Her face broke into a smile although her eyes looked sad.

It was a casual relationship that lasted about six months, as Rose was one of many we'd see in our weekly visits. On our last visit with Rose, she was in bed, her head flung back on her pillow, her eyes closed and mouth open. "Not good," said her sister. I put my hand on her arm and said a silent prayer. Bella sniffed around under the bed looking for crumbs. We left. The following week, Rose's bed was empty and all her belongings, even the plants from the windowsill, were gone. Just to make sure, I asked the nurse and was told that Rose had passed a few days earlier.

At the end of Rose's life, a dog entered her room. A forty-pound whippet, lab, and terrier mix—a rescue from Puerto Rico and an unlikely therapy dog because she survived a dangerous place as a puppy and had issues. These issues included not liking many other dogs; hating to have her head patted; a huge phobia of thunder, fireworks, and gunshots; and a general fearfulness—and added to that is her terrier "I know best" attitude. But despite all this, or maybe because of it, Bella is good at her job. She shows up, she's present, and in ways that are very hard to describe, she reaches people. She does something. She breaks through loneliness and fear.

And she's a busy working girl. She has helped special needs children overcome their fear of dogs and relax while reading a book. In the hospital, she has distracted patients during procedures or nudged them into turning one of those corners that make hard times a little easier. She knows how to cheer up nursing home residents or help college students relax before exams. And despite a lot of training, she reminds me every day that she's a dog. She obeys (mostly), she knows the routine, but she clearly has her own ideas about things and will not, for example, stand still if a nurse comes rushing toward her proclaiming in a high-pitched voice, "Oh, look! A dog!"

So what difference did Bella make for Rose? The first part of the answer is joy—just by entering the room, Bella made Rose smile. She brightened her day. She was something different in an endless routine as Rose's body and mind failed. Bella also provided primal comfort and acceptance. Bella didn't care if Rose could talk, or get hung up on what she was supposed to be, or worry about the future. And through this, Bella told Rose that she would be all right, that she was not alone. For Rose, and for all the lives touched by Bella, this unlikely therapy dog served as a bridge to whatever came next. At the end, there was a dog.

If this sounds like a tall order for an ordinary dog, follow any therapy dog down the hall in a hospital and watch the faces of the people who pass you. They light up—they beam—sadness, distraction, fear, stress, busyness, all but melt away. Animals—dogs in particular—have a powerful effect on us and are ambassadors of the here and now. And yes, some people aren't wild about dogs, and that's fine. One of my favorite patients in the nursing home, Beverly, only touched Bella after seeing her weekly for more than a year, and most of the time, Beverly only looked at me, not her. But that's okay because we're a team. We complement each other and enable each other to do work that neither of us could do alone.

A quick note on "work": this is volunteer work, but having been raised to believe that work is really important, plus being a type A—like Bella—I like to go to work. When I speak this word, she looks for her leash, the red one with little white bones on it that she received when certified as a therapy dog. We have a job and we do it—week after week. Together we go to places where people are sick, lonely, afraid—or in the case of the school children, living with a disability or learning challenge. Sometimes I do the talking, other times Bella is in the forefront; she's the one who curls up in bed with a teenager in the hospital who is terrified to be there. We follow and learn from each other.

Organized in alternating chapters—Bella's rescue and training interspersed with her work as a certified therapy dog—I hope to show you what it takes for these extraordinary animals to become therapy dogs and how they affect patients in nursing homes and hospitals and help children feel excited about learning. This is not a training manual, but a true story about Bella and the work she does. My personal story is another thread in this narrative—I discovered how working with Bella helped me through losing my job, selling our house, and moving to another state to start over at age sixty-five. In the early chapters, there is a five-year gap between Bella's training and her certification, but as the book evolves, these two pieces come together. Join us in our adventure—it's an amazing journey.

PART I: EARLY DAYS

Chapter 1

WHAT WERE WE THINKING?

May 2007
Yardley, Pennsylvania

Angus died. He was our first dog; a collie-shepherd mix. At sixteen, he was the gentlest and most loving companion. We had adopted him from the Bucks County SPCA when he was just a year old. For me, it was love at first sight—I saw his face, his beautiful tri-color coat, and even though he pulled and was a bit wild when we took him out for a walk, I wouldn't return him to his pen out of fear someone else would get him. My husband, Bob, and our five-year-old son, Peter, walked another dog while Angus and I hung out in the parking lot. It was a warm April day and I was excited, as I hadn't had a dog since I was a child.

We'd always wanted a dog, but having lived in New York City for the first seven years of our marriage, we didn't want the hassle of caring for a dog. When we moved to Pennsylvania, we had so many expenses that we knew it wasn't the right time. But eventually, all the pieces fell into place.

"This the one you want?" asked Bob. I didn't have to answer—my face said it all. Peter patted him and we noticed how gentle the dog without a name was. He was a stray who had been picked up on the side of the road. He had already been at the shelter long enough to be adopted, and after paying fifty dollars and signing a contract that we would get him neutered within two weeks (there was a fifty-dollar returnable deposit we had to pay for, too), we put the dog in the back of our station wagon and drove to the store to pick up supplies. I stayed in the car to keep him company while Bob and Peter did the shopping.

Even at the end of his life, Angus showed the same sweetness we had seen in him at the shelter. If it was too difficult for him to get up to greet us, he'd lift his head and wag his tail like mad. His face was expressive, too—large brown eyes that shone with love. But as his organs failed, we knew we had to make the impossible decision to put him down.

We carried him to the car, both of us weeping, and Bob said, "I can't do this."

I replied, "But we have to. He's suffering and isn't going to get better. If there's any hope, the vet will tell us."

It was a Sunday in June, so we had to go to the emergency veterinary services. We carried Angus into the examining room on his bed and put him gently on the floor. The vet came in and listened to his heart and other vital signs and told us we were doing the right thing. "His organs are shutting down. Take as long as you like." He left the room, and Bob and I folded ourselves around Angus, patting and talking to him. He didn't seem afraid—always trusting us. After what felt like a long time, I asked Bob if we should have the vet come back in with the injection. He couldn't talk, but nodded. It was peaceful and quick and then I had to leave the room. Bob stayed behind as I wept in the lobby and took care of the paperwork and bill. When he finally came out of the room, we decided we couldn't go home—too many things reminded us of him. So we drove to the canal towpath that we had walked so many times with Angus, and this time we walked by ourselves. It felt awful. Finally, we went home and I put away his belongings.

Losing him was so hard that we waited almost a year before considering another dog. Spring was on its way again, and Bob, being a college professor, had four months of free time—the perfect opportunity to train a dog. This was 2007.

We went back to the Bucks County SPCA where we had found Angus, but they didn't have many dogs, and the only one we thought might work couldn't be released, as he had behavioral issues and needed additional testing. Peter was by now in college, but my daughter had a one-year-old child and lived nearby, so we wanted to make sure our new dog would be safe around children. We stood in the parking lot, missing Angus even more acutely.

Bob said, "We won't find another dog like him." I agreed, but then said, "He was a bit wild when we first got him. It took time for us to figure it all out. Can't we do that again?"

Bob nodded, not exactly a yes, and we decided to drive over to St. Hubert's Animal Welfare Center in New Jersey, as the daughter of a woman I worked with was connected with that shelter and had told her mother they had lots of puppies. We had seen photos of them online and had picked out a cute brown one to investigate.

An hour later at St. Hubert's, a young woman named Kim greeted us and took us back to the outdoor runs where the puppies were. We asked to see the brown one and she brought him out to a fenced-in yard where we could play with him. Bob and I sat down on the grass and the puppy sniffed our sneakers and walked away. We had filled out a long form, and Kim had asked us a wide range of questions about what we wanted. After a few minutes she said, "This isn't the dog for you. He's not that interested in people."

We agreed and went back to look at the others. There were two white puppies, brother and sister in pens next to each other, each with sweet faces and freckles on their noses. Bob instantly bonded with the larger one, the female, while I hung back, not sure about either one of them. I was disappointed that the first puppy hadn't worked out and was wondering if we were nuts to even think of a puppy at our age (late fifties, early sixties).

But when we sat on the grass with this one, she stayed with us and seemed curious about who we were. After sniffing around for a few minutes, she sat down on top of Bob's foot. She was only twenty pounds and had been rescued from Puerto Rico. She and about forty other dogs had been flown to Newark Airport, as St. Hubert's helped other shelters that were overrun and her chances of being adopted here were much better.

"How old is she?" I asked.

"The vet thinks she and her brother are between three-and-a-half to four months old," said Kim.

Bob and I talked for a while, and Kim let us bring her into the room where the cats were in cages to see how she'd do, since we had a cat, Henry. She sniffed around the room with her ears up, but didn't lunge at the cages or bark, so we figured she'd be all right.

We decided to have lunch at a diner next door and promised we'd come back either way. We needed time. All I remember of that lunch is that I ate a Greek salad and vacillated wildly back and forth—one moment telling Bob how cute she was, and the next, wondering what on earth we were doing.

Cuteness won out. Her face got us—and her story. She had been pulled off of Dead Dog Beach at about two months old and she needed a home. Why not us? In hindsight, I could give you a pretty good list of reasons not to adopt her, but we did it anyway. We bought a crate and put her in it in the back of the car, but she was so scared and howling so loudly that we pulled over and let her sit in the back seat. The whining continued and I told Bob to pull over again, thinking maybe she had to do her business. I walked her in the grass at the side of the road but she wouldn't do anything. About five miles later, she pooped all over the back of the car. Again we pulled over and got the mess cleaned up. Finally, we arrived home and we took her out to our fenced-in backyard and stood with her in the sun. She was so scared that she didn't take more than a step or two away from us. Bob held her in his arms, and I took their picture.

Our adventure had begun.

Chapter 2

THIS IS A CRAZY PLACE: HOSPITAL ORIENTATION

December 2011–January 2012
St. Mary Medical Center, Langhorne, Pennsylvania

Cathy and her dog, Brandon, as well as another neighbor, Kim, and her dog, Lela, had been taking agility classes with us, but it was Cathy's idea to switch to therapy dog work. The moment she mentioned it, I knew this was exactly what I wanted to do with Bella. I was done with weave poles, tunnels, and agility trials. After two good years of training, I still didn't feel that either Bella or I fit. We were never a part of the purebred dog owners group, and I was no longer willing to spend every Saturday driving to agility trials where there was endless waiting combined with heart-stopping panic and worrying about all the rules. All this anxiety crested when they called, "Bella, All American!"—a very nice way of saying "mixed breed"—and we charged through the obstacles, me praying that Bella would remember her hours of training and not shoot through a tunnel the wrong way or jump off the teeter. I enjoyed seeing the dogs who did this beautifully, but given my competitive nature, I felt defensive about Bella's wild streak and was not willing to put in the work that might make her more like them. In the few trials we did do, I ended up mad at the judges, as well as disappointed in Bella and myself. The experience left a bad taste in my mouth, and I couldn't deal with more loss now that I had been notified that the job I'd had for the past sixteen years would be ending in a few weeks.

Cathy had done all the research and had connected with David, who had started a therapy dog program at our local hospital in Pennsylvania a few years earlier. He worked as a jeweler and had a busy schedule, so it took a few weeks to pin him down. About ten years earlier, he'd had a heart attack, and during his long convalescence, his wife brought his two dogs into the hospital. Although he still had a long road ahead of him, he noticed the dogs made him feel better, and that when he walked them around the ward, the other patients wanted to see them. This was around 2000 or 2002, and back then, dogs and hospitals were not generally seen as an acceptable pairing. Administrators worried about germs and about dogs upsetting patients, liability issues, and so on.

But David had experienced firsthand what it was like to have dogs as part of his healing regimen, and he fought hard to have them admitted to this hospital. At first, he and the other volunteers were only allowed in waiting rooms, and then in just a few other places. But by the time Cathy and I started volunteering, we could go pretty much everywhere except maternity, surgery, or into rooms with patients who had communicable diseases or compromised immune systems.

At 7 p.m. one cold December night, Cathy and I drove to the hospital together, gave the dogs a few minutes to do their business on the frozen grass, and then had the surreal experience of walking into the hospital with two dogs. People stopped dead in their tracks. Some did a double take. Others backed away. Cathy and I smiled and tried to look as if we knew what we were doing. We went to the main desk and told the woman that we were meeting David for our therapy dog orientation. She told us to wait over by the chairs. Bella looked around, clearly on high alert, while Brandon—always Mr. Cool—sat quietly by Cathy's feet.

A few minutes later, David came into the hospital with his two Portuguese water dogs, and I saw the hair stand up along Bella's back. I kept her behind Brandon, who also had issues with other dogs, but who at this moment seemed relaxed and happy. We were now a pack of four dogs and three people, and I was excited for the first time in months. Even though we hadn't done anything, I felt a sense of purpose and belonging.

"Let's go up to the fourth floor," said David.

We followed him and filled up much of the elevator. I noticed a few older people who were waiting for the elevator decided to wait for the next one. Bella had never been in an elevator but didn't seem to mind. I had a firm hold on her leash, as I didn't want her near David's dogs. They ignored her and acted as if nothing special was going on.

We quickly learned the protocol: pick a floor, go to the nurse's station, and ask if any patients would like a visit from a dog. Check the signs on each door to make sure we were allowed in. Ask the patient if he or she would like a visit from a dog. If yes, spray the bottom of the dogs' feet with a mild disinfectant, squirt some on our own hands from one of the foam dispensers outside the patient's room, and walk over to the bed, being very careful not to trip over any tubes or other medical equipment. Then introduce the dogs:

"This is Bella and Brandon and they're here to visit."

See if the patient wants to pat them, or if they'd prefer that the dogs put their front paws on the bed, or in special occasions, jump up on the bed. (I couldn't believe the hospital allowed this.)

Cathy and I followed David and glanced at each other as we left each patient's room. Neither of us were sure we could do this. And to top it off, I was convinced that I would get lost in this huge, rambling hospital and would never find my way back to the main lobby. I tried to pay attention, but most of all, I was overcome by seeing, for the first time, the powerful effect the dogs had. Tiredness became excitement, isolation was replaced with companionship, and loneliness was forgotten. Brandon sauntered into these rooms, looked casually around, and if we stayed long enough, he sat down. Why not take a little rest? Bella, on the other hand, was nervous. There were strange noises and stranger smells, and she was reluctant to get near the beds and wheelchairs. She stuck very close to my legs and gave Brandon a lick on the mouth when we were out in the hallway.

"Get the basic idea?" asked David after we had seen a half-dozen patients.

Cathy and I nodded.

"Some patients won't want to see you, and you can always ask at the nurse's station if there is anyone you should make sure to visit."

He led us to the elevator and we returned to the ground floor. He showed us where the volunteer office was and where to sign in and out. They had bottles of spray for the dogs and he told us to take one. He reminded us of the cardinal rule: we were never to ask about a patient's condition. We weren't there to offer advice, and we never talked about the patients unless there was an issue that needed to be reported to a nurse or the volunteer supervisor.

"You'll also be getting special leashes. St. Mary's doesn't use the volunteer jackets for pet therapy work, but you'll have a nice blue leash with St. Mary Medical Center written on it. Make sure to use that and to wear your name tags. You can wear your dogs' name tags, too, or clip them to their collars."

There was so much to remember. We thanked David, put on our jackets and gloves, and headed out into the cold night.

"Got that?" I asked Cathy as both dogs squatted in the brittle grass. We burst out laughing.

"Good thing we're doing this together," said Cathy, and I agreed. I wasn't a shy person, but this felt overwhelming and we were both afraid of doing something wrong.

Brandon and Bella were happy to be outside. They sniffed their way to the car and we drove home. Cathy and I told the volunteer office that we would come every Monday at 1 p.m., starting in January. I was grateful for this structure; I didn't know what I was going to do without work. It was going to be very strange to have all this free time. Well-meaning friends told me that everything was happening for a reason, but I was never a big fan of that concept. I couldn't find a reason for my job loss that made sense to me, and although I could guess why my name was on the list, I was still in that hurt, "why me" phase and wasn't sure how to break out of it. To top it all off, a career coach losing her job was supremely ironic—like a doctor getting sick.

I loved my work, but I was beginning to realize I had outgrown the industry I'd been in for sixteen years. I had grown up in the industry when personal attention and deep relationships were valued, but at age sixty-five, it was clear that I had never adjusted to the increasing pressure to see more clients and give them less time. So I wasn't only mourning my job loss, but all that had been lost over the past few years.

"This was the best," said Cathy as she dropped me off. I agreed. It really was. I was deeply grateful to have something new and hopeful in my life. I was also grateful for her.

I gave her a big hug.

Chapter 3

THE CAT IS NOT A SNACK

June 2007
Yardley, Pennsylvania

The crate we'd bought saved our life. Bella had never been in a home and was *wild*. She flew through the air at warp speed, crashed into furniture, jumped over chairs, and only focused on two things: digging and chewing. She ate one of my leather sandals. She devoured a decorative pillow and chewed through the mat and towels in her crate. Our backyard looked like a moonscape from Bella's craters. She was so out of control that we had to keep her on the leash in the house, and walking her was a lesson in frustration. She pulled, veered, stopped abruptly, and was afraid of plastic bags and the ceramic frog in our front garden that Bob's mother had made for us.

I worked from home two days a week and was in the office for the other three, but poor Bob, who was off for the summer, got to be with Bella every day. He was on the brink of a meltdown. And while we both knew it was unfair, we couldn't help but compare her to Angus—our sixteen-year-old mellow dog who, even in his youth, couldn't touch Bella's energy. It was like having another species in our home—something completely foreign and destructive.

Henry, our three-year-old cat, also a rescue, liked to think he was a dog and was unafraid of this whirling dervish. This wasn't really smart on his part—we had no idea what Bella would do around him. On about our fifth day with Bella, I was upstairs getting ready for work and I heard Bella tearing through the house after Henry. Her nails slid on the hardwood floors, and I heard an occasional crash as she collided with anything that got in her way.

"Bob!" I shouted. "What's going on?"

"Thought I'd see how they work it out themselves."

"Are you kidding?"

I ran downstairs half-dressed to find Bella barking at the couch. Henry had wisely gotten himself under it where she couldn't reach him.

"Crate time," I told her, putting her in the crate with a treat. "Henry is not a snack. You can play but you can't hurt him."

She looked at me with her deep brown eyes, as if saying "Really?"

"Be a good girl and have a little quiet time."

She flopped down on her side and chewed on the thick mat that lined the bottom of the crate. I ran back upstairs, finished getting ready for work, and gave Bob a kiss.

"Hang in there," I told him. "It's going to take time."

I could see from his face that he was having serious doubts. We both were.

"I'll do some research at lunch time," I told him, "and find an obedience class. Other people make it through this."

"Maybe they use drugs," muttered Bob.

"For the dog or for themselves?" I asked.

"Let's go for both."

As I drove to work, I realized we were in for a long, slow process—one with uncertain outcomes. But I also knew we were going to do it—we were going to make it work. There was nothing sweeter than Bella curled up on top of Bob, her pink belly facing the ceiling, her long thin legs stretched straight up in the air.

Next challenge: housebreaking. Kim from St. Hubert's had said to take her outside of the crate immediately and to use an authoritative command such as "Do your business." We tried it and sometimes it worked. But to get to the back door, we had to go through the family room, which had wall-to-wall carpeting, and Bella often peed a few paces from the door.

"No!" we shouted, and dragged her outside, using the "Do your business" command. I spent a lot of time on my hands and knees with a miracle spray that was supposed to break down the enzymes of dog pee. One good thing—she hadn't pooped in the house.

Our close neighbors, Jim and Jodi, also had a new puppy, Cooper, a yellow lab. Jodi and I decided to hire a dog trainer to come once a week to teach our wild puppies how to behave. The problem was, Bella was so excited to be with Cooper in every session that she didn't pay any attention to the basic commands like sit, stay, or heel. She thought it was play time and hurled herself underneath Cooper, biting at his chest and face. Cooper was happy to go along with this plan, until finally Jodi and I got them separated.

We had homework: Bella—sit. Bella—stay. Bella—come. We used treats as lures and sometimes they worked. Bella—heel. We practiced in the house and in the backyard. When she pulled when we were out walking, I stopped and didn't continue until she walked nicely beside me with a loose leash. It took forever. I wished she could be off-leash the way Angus always was; it was so frustrating being tethered to this high-voltage creature. I had expected training to be easy. I had expected quick results. I wanted her to get an A from the trainer. It didn't happen.

I made up a poem to help myself get through it. It started with: "There is nothing merrier than a crazy little terrier." Actually, that's as far as I got except that I changed the word *crazy* to *wild*, or *stubborn*, or *head-strong*. It was my mantra. I repeated it endlessly—in my head, out loud, sometimes turning it into a song. This silly poem helped me realize that Bella and I were a lot alike; and although I wouldn't admit it, I admired her fierce independence and determination.

On one particular walk, Bob and I were struggling up a hill in our neighborhood with Bella darting this way and that when we saw another couple and their dog walking behind us. It was Cathy, John, and Brandon, and luckily for us, the two dogs liked each other right away. Cathy saw the discouragement in our faces and told us not to worry—that it took about two years for a dog to settle down and really get it.

"Are you kidding?" I asked. "Two years?"

Cathy looked at John, who nodded. "Yes—that's about right. Of course it gets easier along the way, too."

Bob and I groaned.

"You'll make it," said Cathy, the eternal optimist. "Just look at how cute she is!"

And she was right—Bella was really cute with pink spots on her nose and a face that radiated curiosity and sweetness. As we walked along together, we shared our list of grievances, and John suggested getting an Easy Walk harness so that Bella couldn't drag us down the street. We'd never heard of such a thing, but were ready to try anything that made walking easier. Bella often got three good walks a day—our desperate attempt to tire her out.

We bought the harness, and witnessed a miracle. The harness clasp was on the chest, not the back, so that if the dog pulled, he or she was forced to turn into you and therefore couldn't keep moving. It may have seemed like a small thing, but it saved us from constant frustration, from that terrier drive and leader-of-the-pack mentality. It wasn't perfect—Bella still didn't understand the concept of walking along beside us—but it was a huge help. Maybe we would make it after all.

Chapter 4

THE INFUSION ROOM

February 2012
St. Mary Medical Center, Langhorne, Pennsylvania

My best friend from college, Nancy, had been diagnosed with breast cancer. It seemed like a bad dream. Unreal. She didn't tell me about it for weeks. And hanging over her was the shadow of her mother's early death from cancer at age fifty-two. Nancy and I lived several hours from each other, so I couldn't take Bella to see her, but in her honor and to get a glimpse of what she was going through, I decided that Bella and I would visit the Cancer Center in the hospital every week.

Cathy and Brandon were busy on our first visit to the Cancer Center, so Bella and I were on our own. We walked down a long, carpeted hallway, the sun streaming in floor-to-ceiling windows. It was the dead of winter and the sun felt wonderful. We moved through the glass doors into the Cancer Center and the woman behind the desk tried to hide her surprise.

I introduced myself and told her that Bella was a therapy dog and that we'd wanted to visit the infusion room. I couldn't hide my pride as I said "therapy dog." It had been five years with so many ups and downs, so many times when I wasn't sure she'd pass her tests, but we had finally made it.

"May I pet her?" she asked, coming out from behind the desk.

"She's a little shy," I explained, as Bella backed up. "Head-shy."

"Oh, she doesn't like me," said the woman.

"No, that's not it. She's new to this work and it's going to take time, that's all. We plan to come every week so she'll get used to you." Then I added, as though this explained everything, "She's a rescue." I hoped that the image of a dog abandoned or abused would give Bella permission to be afraid, although I knew so little of what happened to her in Puerto Rico that I realized this was hardly an excuse.

The receptionist offered to show us around, starting with a waiting room made up of comfortable chairs, potted plants, and bright art work. I couldn't tell if the people sitting there were patients or families waiting for patients. Off to the side was a gurney where a young man lay. He was covered by a white blanket and was fast asleep. I stared at his face—he was so young and yet looked ravaged—all bones and sunken flesh.

For the first time it occurred to me that this wasn't going to be easy, that I was entering uncharted territory. This was a new world to me where my instincts—to touch him, find out about him, ask if he'd make it—weren't allowed. I turned away, but his face stayed with me for weeks.

"Here's the infusion room," said my guide, and I noticed a row of reclining chairs lined up along the length of the room. All the chairs were filled and everyone was connected to an IV. A few were asleep, one or two were reading, and the rest looked at Bella as if they'd never seen a dog in their lives. The nurses behind the desk looked startled, but the receptionist quickly introduced Bella and explained to them that she would be visiting on a weekly basis.

"Good girl," I said to her, to cover my nervousness. We approached the first chair.

"Would you like to see Bella?" I asked.

A woman about my age nodded. "She looks sweet. Is she a puppy?"

"No, she's five, but we've had her since she was about four months old."

Then I realized we had a logistical problem. The patients couldn't reach her, so very carefully I had Bella put her front paws on the seat of the chair. I lured her into this position with a treat and then asked the woman if she'd like to give Bella one. She nodded and we had our first routine worked out.

We worked our way down the line of chairs, being careful not to touch the tubing that was carrying the chemo from the IVs to the patients. One woman had beautiful red socks with green Christmas trees on them. I admired them and, after a few weeks, came to look forward to seeing her collection. An elderly man told me about his dog—turns out this was a dog he had when he was in his twenties—and a few others wanted to know about Bella—what breed she was, who trained her, where she came from, whether or not she was my dog, and how she became a therapy dog. I realized her story was part of the healing. She was a canine Cinderella, or as one patient put it: "She hit the jackpot!"

The nurses were wary, and I was careful to stay out of their way and to always check in with them. I understood they were working and we were extra, like icing on the cake. But by our third visit to the Cancer Center, they had become our biggest advocates; they started asking the patients themselves if they'd like to see Bella. Once Brandon joined us, they fussed over him just as much. He was so handsome—a collie, Rottweiler mix, all soft fur with a swaying gait that seemed to say *aren't you lucky to see me?* Bella adored him, and on our way out of the infusion room, she often licked his mouth—a sign of joy and submission. This made some of the patients laugh.

"True love," I told them. "She's crazy about Brandon."

Like many males, he also liked the attention, but didn't let on that it mattered in the least.

As Cathy and the dogs and I returned week after week, we often saw the same patients. Some looked the same, but others became more thin and haggard. I dreaded seeing their chairs empty, knowing that this horrible disease may have won out despite all their efforts. But we could never ask or discuss medical issues. We showed up, observed, let the dogs do their thing, and because we were now part of the routine of this place, we told the patients if we had to skip a week. That was it. I thought of my friend Nancy going through this week after week, and my cousin Linda who died of breast cancer at barely fifty, leaving behind her husband and two teenage daughters.

But the dogs made seeing this okay. They brought so much joy into the room that they balanced out the fear and sadness. After only a few months, this place—this front line of a terrible battle—felt normal. In fact, it had become my favorite place in the hospital.

Every week, before we left the hospital, Cathy and I went to the cafeteria. As volunteers, we were given vouchers worth five dollars. One of us stood in the hall with the dogs, who weren't allowed in the cafeteria, and the other got drinks and snacks. Then we took our stash to the volunteer office and had a little party, talking over who we visited, how it went, and what we learned. Bella and Brandon were very interested in this part, as food was involved, and after helping us eat the snacks, they often stretched out under the table and fell asleep.

I was lucky to be with someone like Cathy. She was warm, funny, accepting, and excellent company. She was a freelance clothing designer of outerwear, and so she not only had a flexible schedule, but also understood on a deep and personal level what it was like to be out of work. I realized much later, after we had moved and were no longer working with Cathy and Brandon, what a gift that time with her had been.

I thought Bella had similar feelings about Brandon and much preferred visiting the hospital with him rather than with just me. Together they were a pack—somehow more than two dogs. They generated even more attention from staff, families, and patients than they did individually, and they quickly learned that one dog could approach the bed, or wheelchair, while the other held back, waiting for his or her turn. I was convinced they learned from each other, Bella picking up on Brandon's laissez-faire attitude, he on her energy and enthusiasm. And once we were back in the hall, they were just dogs—curious, strolling along together, somehow making sense of this place that was packed with strange noises, stranger smells, and lots of activity.

🐾 🐾

I never liked to admit it, but there were days when I was lost. When the world felt confusing and I wasn't sure what to do, who I was, or what was next. It's a cliché to say that change is difficult, but there I was at age sixty-five, having lost my job of sixteen years, and I was resentful. Why did they let me go? Why couldn't I have turned in my resignation when we were ready to move out of the area? Why didn't anyone I worked with remember me? No one had called, or emailed me, or checked in to see how I was doing. I felt as if I had died. As if that wasn't enough, we were in the middle of trying to sell our house where we had raised our children and built a community for the past twenty-four years. The day the For Sale sign went up in January, I flipped out. This was my house, my neighborhood, my trees, my yard. But without selling it, we couldn't move. Bob was still working so he couldn't dwell on it. But I wasn't working, so I did.

On good days, I remembered our plan. I remembered that we were moving to a special place. We would be living near a salt cove just outside the most beautiful New England fishing village. We had a house there that we bought four years ago and it already felt like home. The sea breeze and salt air were amazing, there was a rack down by the water for our kayaks, and the neighborhood was really a park. But we didn't know what it would be like to actually live there. And what about work? What would I do? How would I find a job?

Bob planned on retiring and was so close he could practically taste it. He was so excited, so ready for a new chapter. My job seemed to be to get rid of stuff so that our move would be easier, to get Bella and Henry out of the house every time there was a showing, and to keep the house spotless. I bought fluffy white towels that we never used. I swept things into drawers and closets. I removed our photographs. I got rid of the furniture that Henry had destroyed with his sharp claws. In short, I made our home not really our home. I was at the whim of realtors and their clients. I had no job to go to. I wasn't part of a company. My car knew the way to the office but I couldn't go there.

I obsessed about strange things. For example, a man was parking his car across the street from our driveway so he didn't have to pay the one-dollar fee in the lot around the corner by the train station. At first it was nothing. Then I got angry that his car was there. Then I happened to run into him one morning while walking Bella.

"Excuse me," I said, in my loud, I-know-what-I'm-doing voice. His eyebrows shot up.

"You taking the train?"

He hesitated then nodded.

"Why don't you park in the lot? This is a dangerous corner."

He didn't answer.

"Don't park here," I said, preparing to keep walking.

"No sign that says I can't."

"That doesn't mean it's a good idea!" and I left, smoke curling from the top of my head, fantasizing about leaving dog poop on the hood of his car.

Bella followed me, and I didn't enjoy or even see anything on our walk. When we got back to the house, I called the police and told them his car was a nuisance. An exit from the bank was located just beyond his car, so cars coming down our street didn't have a clear view. The policeman humored me for about a minute and told me he would check it out, but said there was nothing he could do if it was a legal spot.

Later, when Bob got home, I told him how mad I was. I told him I called the police.

"You what?" he asked. "Why?"

"Because," I shouted. "It's wrong! He shouldn't be there."

"But Jean, it doesn't really matter, does it? It's not your job."

"Yes it is!" And I burst into tears.

Bob took me in his arms, and for the first time since I was let go, I cried. I had been so proud of my work, the relationships I built with my clients, the classes I designed, the teams I facilitated, and my book on how to recover from job loss. One former client—one of the few people who had reached out to me—said a funny thing: "Jean, did you read your own book? You know better than anyone how to get through this."

"This sucks," I said into Bob's shoulder.

"It does, but once we move, you're going to find other work. You always have."

I thanked him, but what I was really thinking was *I don't want to! I want my old job back!*

My friends asked me how I was doing and I told them I was fine. I was efficient. I got stuff done, and I also had a book deadline to meet, so I did have work. There were days when I wondered where I belonged, moments when I was sure I'd been put out to pasture and would never work again. Henry curled up on my lap and Bella sat under my desk, hoping for a walk. But every Monday, Bella and I went to the hospital with Cathy and Brandon, and that bright spot, that one chance to focus on something else, pulled me through.

Chapter 5

BABY STEPS

July 2007
Yardley, Pennsylvania

It's hard to remember now how wild Bella was. In those early days, everything was unsettled. The one amazing thing she learned right away, though, was not to eat Henry's food. She somehow understood that she could only eat out of her own dish—but if one tiny speck of cat food fell from Henry's dish onto the floor, then it belonged to Bella. She was the cleaner-upper.

Our early successes included getting her to sit on command, to go into her crate without a struggle (which was always made easier by a treat), and to walk on our left side without darting in front of us. The pulling continued, even with the Easy Walk harness, but was bearable. Although I knew to stop walking every time she pulled on her leash, I was too impatient to keep up this routine, so Bella pulled and I yanked her back and we lurched down the street during every walk.

Having grown up in the country where we had thirteen acres of woods and no nearby neighbors or busy streets, I believed that dogs should be able to run free—a leash was a necessary tool, but not one that should be used all the time. When we walked Angus, we carried his leash with us but didn't put it on unless we were worried about a busy part of the road or another dog.

"Can you imagine what she'd do if you let her go?" Bob asked once.

With her dominant Whippet genes, she'd be gone in a flash. But at least she had our backyard to run in and was getting to be friends with Cooper, Brandon, and another neighborhood dog, Lela. Lela was so well trained that Kim could open her car dog and Lela would wait beside the car. And when we went hiking together, Lela was off-leash. Was that too crazy a goal to hope for? Would I ever be able to trust Bella like that? Bella was only a puppy, while Lela was three, and I knew that made a huge difference. Another challenge was her reaction to other dogs: there was no middle ground, no neutral. Bella loved them or she hated them. Two houses down from us lived a couple with German Shepherds—large, aggressive dogs. The man who had them thought of himself as the Dog Whisperer and never had them on leashes. Walking by his house was a challenge. I often pulled Bella to the other side of the street and tried to get past his house without the two animals charging us. When I saw them coming, I screamed: "Get your dogs! Get them out of here!" which had mixed results. Sometimes he came out of his house and gave a loud whistle and they returned, other times he was out of ear shot and did nothing. Bella bared her teeth and tried to bite them, while I did my best to stay between her and them and kept shouting, "Go home!" I'm sure I made things worse.

Which was why, when this man suggested one day that the dogs "play" together, I agreed. I thought that if they got to know each other, we'd be spared our walk-by attacks. He brought over the younger male—a beautiful, dark Shepherd who immediately went for Bella's hind end. She had other ideas about how to meet and greet and ran as fast as she could. He charged, flipped her into the air, and pinned her down.

"This isn't good," I said, hyperventilating.

"Don't worry," said the neighbor, watching his dog like a proud parent, "they're just establishing dominance."

"Bella, here!" I shouted, once she wiggled out from under this huge animal.

She ran and hid behind my legs, the other dog in hot pursuit.

"No!" I told him. Again, useless and no doubt making everyone more tense.

After a few more agonizing minutes of this, I told the neighbor that this was enough for now. Bella was small, and his dog, while well-meaning, was too rough.

"You have to let dogs be part of the pack," he said.

I wanted to bite him, and say "Not your pack!"

But I managed to thank him for stopping by, and I'm not sure who was more relieved to see them go—Bella or me.

🐾 🐾

Our classes with Trish, the dog trainer, continued on a weekly basis. We practiced walking with a loose leash; commands such as *sit, stay, right here* or *come*, as well as useful ones like *in your crate*, and *do your business*. The good news—Bella was smart. The not-so-good news—she had so much energy and such a limited attention span that she was like someone with a severe learning disability. Every day we practiced. When we were out walking and saw another dog coming toward us—one of many she disliked— we introduced the *leave it* command. This meant she should ignore the dog and continue her walk as though nothing were happening. It was a good idea in theory, but Bella had other ideas; her hackles rose a good three inches, she bared her teeth, growled, and lunged at the passing intruder.

"No!" I told her, hanging on to the leash, struggling to prevent a dog fight.

I told Trish, the trainer, about this, and she suggested more practice and taking her to places like PetSmart where she would have to interact with strange dogs. I didn't need to think about this for more than a minute to know that Bella wasn't ready. Trish sure knew a lot more than I did about dog training, but I knew Bella better. What I didn't realize, because I'd never had a puppy before, was that they grow up quickly. By the time Bella was almost a year old (we adopted her in May when she was about four months old), she began to understand and finally passed her test with Trish. We were given a bright green certificate that read, "Bella Baur has successfully fulfilled all the requirements necessary to complete PUPPY LEVEL I EDUCATION, December 12, 2007."

Because I was the one doing the training with her, she got my last name. Oh, boy! My goals at this point were simple: to make her more like Angus—a polite, well-trained dog. A dog you could trust. I tried not to compare her to Cooper, who was more mellow and loved everyone. But then I remembered where she came from, and in a handout from Trish about puppy development, I saw that the early weeks of a puppy's life were critical. They shouldn't be removed from their mother or litter mates, and they should be introduced to humans carefully and should not be exposed to loud noises, aggressive behavior, or other threats.

Bella's early life, whether born or dumped on Dead Dog Beach in Puerto Rico, was worse than anything in this handout. And while we didn't know the specifics of what happened to her there, we knew enough to assume it was a dreadful place for a puppy. (I picked up a book called *Rescue at Dead Dog Beach* that provided horrific details. It took me a month to read it as it gave me nightmares.) I asked the shelter in New Jersey how they got Bella and learned that they partnered with a group in Puerto Rico called Amigos de los Animales PR (Friends of Animals Puerto Rico.) The name Mary Eldergill was on Bella's inoculation records — the woman who had saved Bella and two of her siblings from the beach. She fostered them in her home while Amigos de los Animales PR made arrangements for the forty dogs rescued from Dead Dog Beach to be flown to Newark Airport and sheltered at St. Hubert's in North Branch, New Jersey. Upon arrival, she was de-wormed, given her shots, spayed, and micro-chipped. One month after that, she came home with us. That was an awful lot of change for the first four months of a puppy's life. Change and loss. I didn't know what happened to her mother or her siblings except for her brother, who had also been at St. Hubert's. For one fleeting moment, Bob had thought about adopting him, too, but we knew that was a mistake. One puppy was enough.

Give her time, I told myself. *Be patient.* These were not qualities that came easily to me, but I worked on them, as Bella had clearly made her way into my heart.

Chapter 6

DEALING WITH THE UNEXPECTED

March–April 2012
Yardley, Pennsylvania

Just when I thought I had this whole hospital thing down, and that Cathy, Brandon, Bella, and I knew our way around and were doing good work visiting patients, I was accosted by a teenage volunteer, a girl in a blue volunteer jacket. Cathy and Brandon were still chatting in a patient's room, and Bella and I were walking toward the next room, when this young woman came barreling at us. I quickly put myself between her and Bella.

"Hey! Take it easy."

"I want to see your dog," she said, ignoring me.

"You can see her but not like that. You're scaring her."

She circled me and tried to get her hands on Bella. The leash got tangled in my legs.

"Come here!" she shouted. "Let me pet you!"

Bella was quicker than she was, though, and managed to pull away just as one of her hands was ready to slam down on her head.

Now I was angry. "Stop it!" I told her. "You're scaring her. This is not the way to approach a dog."

Something got through.

"Oh," she said, finally still. "But I just wanted to pet her."

"You can pet her, but you've got to be more gentle. She doesn't understand what you want."

Bella was looking at me as if to say, *can we please get out of here?*

"But, but—"

"No. If you'd like to give her a treat, you can squat down and she'll come to you."

"Can't do that. Can't."

Still between her and Bella I asked, "Why not?"

She ducked her head and mumbled, "ADHD."

Now I was stunned. "I'm sorry, but she's small and you're big, so you have to move slowly and then she'll be fine."

The girl gave me one last look and darted down the hall.

Just then Cathy came out of the patient's room. "What happened to you?" she asked. I told her and she laughed. "Well, we'll never be bored here, will we?" And then she leaned down to pat Bella. Bella loved her, even allowing Cathy to touch her head. "She's such a sweetie."

We visited a few more rooms in the unit and then took the elevator up to the oncology ward. On our way to the nurse's station, we passed a room in which several nurses attended to an elderly man. We hesitated, not knowing if we'd be in the way or a help. One of the nurses saw us and said, "Can you come here for a minute?"

"Sure," said Cathy, and we entered the room. The man was agitated, talking about going home, and wouldn't let the nurse put in his IV. Because his bed was so high, he couldn't see the dogs.

"Would you like to see my dog, Bella?" I asked him. He seemed a bit stunned but nodded. At least this was something different.

"Can I put her on the bed?" I asked the nurses and they told me it was fine. So I lifted Bella, careful to put her down gently beside this man. She sniffed his arm and then curled up right beside him. All the fear and tension left the room. He took his other hand and slowly stroked Bella's back.

"Nice dog," he said. "What a good boy."

I didn't correct him about her gender and simply said, "Yes, she is and she's happy to visit you."

While he and I chatted, the nurse got his line in and they thanked us and left. Cathy and I stayed for a while because Bella's warm body pressed up against his was probably the nicest thing that had happened to him in a long while.

We were in our final week before our house closing, and it felt as complicated as planning a major military offensive. We had endless lists of things that had to get done each day as we prepared for the movers to come. It was a poignant time—everything was marked by "last"—the last walk on the canal, the last time at church, the last game of tennis with my group, and so on. In the midst of this countdown, a former client, Kamora, asked me if Bella would come to her Girl Scout Troop, as the girls were working on their Animal Helpers Cadette Badge. I knew it was crazy to say yes because I was supposed to be home packing boxes, but I did it anyway. I said yes because this was an opportunity to see how Bella did in a room full of children—and I was dying to get out of the house.

I told Kamora that the girls couldn't run at her when we came into the room. They needed to sit and let her approach them first. We drove to the nearby town and found the church where the meeting was held. I was amazed by how easily Bella adapted to strange places, sniffing the grass, not at all spooked by walking down long hallways.

"Hey, Jean!" said Kamora, meeting us outside the auditorium. "She's even cuter than you!"

We laughed and she told me a bit about the troop and the work they were doing. When we entered the room, all eyes were on Bella.

"Oh, look!" said several girls, but none moved from their places on the floor.

Kamora told them that I would talk to them for a few minutes about Bella and what she did, and then they would have a chance to pet her.

We went to the front of the room and I told Bella to sit. She did.

"This is Bella" is how I started, telling them where she was born, how long we'd had her, and a bit about all the training she'd had. Then I told them about the hospital and how she made people feel better. No one moved. Some girls looked a little scared, while others were curious.

A little girl, I think from India, raised her hand.

"Yes?" I said.

"Does she do tricks?"

"She can do a few tricks, and I'll show them to you, but a therapy dog is not a circus dog. Bella's job is to help people feel better. We've been going to the hospital every week and visiting patients."

"I was in the hospital!" shouted a pretty blonde girl.

"What happened to you?" I asked.

"I broke my arm."

"That's too bad," I told her, "but wouldn't it have been wonderful if a dog like Bella had been there to make you feel better? Most people are afraid when they end up in the hospital, right?"

The girls nodded. The Indian girl reminded me that she wanted to see tricks.

"Okay. Here are a few."

Bella was watching me intently. I told her to come closer. When she did, I closed my fingers into a fist and she sat.

"How does she know to do that?" asked another girl.

"I taught her."

Then I pointed to the floor and she lay down.

"Here's the really hard one," I told them. "Watch closely."

I put a treat on the top of Bella's paw and told her, "Leave it!"

She waited. Then I picked up the treat, told her, "Good. Take it," and she was allowed to eat the treat.

The girls clapped. Bella the wonder dog.

She stood up and shook her whole body, tail whipping. I had learned to stay clear of that—it hurt when it hit my legs.

"If you'd like to meet Bella, she will come and greet you. But if you'd prefer just to see her but not pet her, that's fine, too. Just let me know as I walk around the room, okay?"

They nodded and Bella then decided that these were her puppies and that the best thing to do was to lick them all on the face. Kamora beamed, and after we'd seen each girl, I asked if they had any questions.

"Why did you pick this dog?" one child asked.

"You know, I think she picked us. When we went to the shelter where she was being cared for, and they let her out of her pen, guess what she did?"

"Ran away?" suggested one girl.

"No, she stayed really close to my husband and me, and then she sat on his foot. She told him with her body that we were the ones she wanted. Isn't that neat?"

They laughed and after a few more questions we left. Walking out down the long hallway, I paused and said to Bella, "Good girl. That was really good work." And then she got one more treat.

I sat in my car for a few minutes before driving home. It'd been nice to see a former client—to connect again to my years as a career coach. But now, both of us were volunteers—Kamora with her troop, and me with Bella. And that was fine. I didn't have to be the counselor anymore; the one with advice and answers. Not just yet. This new me was a little unsure and still worried about finding work. I was still hurt from losing my job, but excited about what was ahead—something that would be a better fit for who I was now. So in the midst of all this change, the one sure thing was that I was willing to partner with Bella and go where we were needed. In just a few days, we would be living in our new home in Connecticut, and I knew that somehow Bella and I would find a way to continue what we started. We were both hooked.

Chapter 7

PROGRESS

Summer–Fall 2007
Yardley, Pennsylvania

Maybe, just like children, it takes a village to raise a dog well. Even before our training with Trish ended, we realized we needed to enroll Bella in doggie daycare. Bob had to go back to work in the fall, and we didn't feel comfortable leaving her in her crate all day on the three days a week I was at work as well. Luckily, a new facility had opened one town over, and we called to find out the details. Bella had to have an interview to be accepted.

"What do you think?" I asked Bob. "Will she make it?"

"Hard to say. I guess it depends on what they expect."

So, like parents taking a child for a college interview, we drove over to Four Paws and entered the main lobby. It smelled of dog and we could hear loud barking from an outside pen. Bella looked nervous and I wondered if she thought we were returning her to a shelter. We were led into a room where a staff member took down our information: her age (not yet a year), her breed (our vet said she was a whippet, lab, terrier mix, but could also be part Mexican Hairless as she had black skin), any issues we knew about (we were a little coy about her reaction to other dogs but shared that she did best with small dogs), and all our contact information.

"I'm going to bring Sadie into the room," she told us, "and we'll see how Bella does with her. Be right back."

I was tense, worried that Bella would try to attack Sadie. I let Bella wander around the room, sniffing all the good smells, and in came Sadie, a beagle-boxer mix. Bella's hair rose and she backed away from Sadie.

"Give them time," said the staff person. "This isn't bad."

Bella did not want Sadie sniffing her hind end and bared her teeth.

Sadie wasn't easily put off and tried again to sniff Bella's hind end. Bella growled, her ears flat against her head. She whipped her body around so that Sadie couldn't get to her.

I made things worse by pulling on the leash, trying to create a safe distance between the two dogs.

Sadie, being considerably larger, came at Bella from the side and tried to push her down to the floor using her huge head as a battering ram.

I couldn't stand it and yanked Bella away from her. "Could we try a smaller dog?" I asked, fearing that it was only seconds before we'd have a dog fight.

"Sure. We can do that."

Sadie left, and Bob and I exhaled. "I wish she liked other dogs the way Cooper does," I told him, still shaken, the mother lion in me on full alert. No one was going to hurt my girl.

"Well," said Bob, always the practical one, "she doesn't. We don't know why, but she just doesn't. And I think Bella is aggressive because she's afraid. Did you see how her ears were back and her tail between her legs?"

"Yes, I saw that, but Sadie was pushy. She didn't get it that Bella didn't want her in her face."

Like most parents, I'd clearly decided that my dog wasn't the real problem. I took a few deep breaths and tried to get my blood pressure back to normal.

When Spark, a toy poodle, was brought into the room, Bella wagged her tail and ran playfully around him. Here was a dog she liked. The staff person was impressed and said, "She'll do fine. When do you want to start?"

We picked a date a week before Bob's classes started so that we could get her used to Four Paws. I promised to bring in her vaccination record and to get a kennel cough shot, as well. We put Bella in the back seat and told her she was a good girl. We were both a little nervous but knew this would be good for her.

Back at home, we made sure she did her business before coming into the house, but let her loose. We only used the crate at night or when we went out. We trusted her, and Henry had learned when it was a really good idea to escape up his cat pole and when it was safe to play. But we never left them alone together—Bella was still too unpredictable—and Henry wasn't smart enough to avoid wrestling with a creature four times his size.

One rainy day when I was working from home, it seemed a bit too quiet, so I went upstairs and found Bella happily lying on our bed, eating the corner of the duvet cover.

"No!" I said sternly. "Bad dog!"

I examined the duvet to see if it could be mended, but it wasn't ripped. I found a hole and a chunk of the material was missing.

"No, Bella, no!" I shouted, angry and frustrated, wondering why on earth she did this.

"What's wrong with you?" I yelled, giving her a whack on the hind end.

She pulled away from me and cowered.

"You are in so much trouble! Let's go!" I yelled.

I grabbed her collar, yanked her off the bed, and chased her downstairs. "Outside!"

I put her outside so that she could think about what she had done and made myself a cup of tea in an effort to calm down. I hated being mad at her. I hated that she got to me. I didn't feel sympathetic—I didn't want to remember that she was only a dog, doing what dogs do. I expected better. I expected her to be like Angus. No, I thought—she should be like me. And then that sounded so crazy that I laughed and my anger dissipated. While the kettle was coming to boil, I checked on her outside and discovered she had used that unsupervised time to dig a nice big hole in the middle of the backyard.

"Oh, my God!" I shouted, but then decided who the hell cared about the craters. Let her dig. Bob read somewhere that dogs didn't like the smell of Listerine, so he filled the pits in the backyard with Listerine. This made our yard smell like a dentist's office, but had the amazing result of preventing Bella from digging where she had already dug. This smart dog, this driven terrier mix, had it all figured out: dig new holes and everything was just fine!

Sometimes at night, Bob and I would look over at each other and say, "I miss Angus." And we really did—especially his calmness and the fact that we could trust him completely. And he would always be our first dog, the one who grew up with our children, the one we loved unconditionally.

"But that took time, right?" I asked Bob, trying desperately to find a ray of hope.

"Some of it, but Angus was different, that's all. This is another creature and we can't compare them."

And then we'd look over at her, curled up on a towel on the couch, her nose tucked under her front paw, her pink ears folded like fortune cookies, and all the frustrations of helping her grow up would melt away. She was a wonderful dog, and instinctively we knew she had a bright future ahead of her. We just had to get her there, that's all.

🐾 🐾

The best part of that summer was our first grandchild, Molly, who turned one year old that July. She learned to walk and was interested in everything. I was Nonna and Bob was Nonno. She couldn't say that yet, but she knew we were people who loved her. And we saw her often enough that she was no longer shy or hesitant with us.

We were careful with Bella, not sure how she would react to this creature who pulled things off shelves, cried, and was pretty much at her eye level. Bella saw that we loved Molly—that the whole world stopped when she visited—and so, while still being a little jealous, she became her four-legged mother. She licked crumbs off Molly's fingers, waited patiently under her high chair, and any chance she got, washed her face with her tongue. Molly's father hadn't been raised with dogs, so we were careful not to make him uncomfortable, but Emily, our daughter, who had Angus as part of her teenage years, thought it would be good for Molly to get to know dogs at an early age.

But if Molly came around a corner in the house and saw Bella, she screamed. An ear-piercing deadly scream. So I taught her to say "sit" (it came out sounding like "shit") and hold up her hand in a fist. Bella obeyed, and Molly's fear dissipated. We practiced this over and over, but put Bella in one of the bedrooms and closed the door when Molly first arrived. Her excitement was a bit overwhelming for a one-year-old. For anyone, really.

Later in the fall, when Bella had adjusted to going to Four Paws twice a week, I signed up for an obedience class held at their facility. Jody and Cooper were taking the class, too, so we drove over together and then lined up in a circle in a large room. The instructor had clear goals for us: the dogs had to learn to walk on a loose leash, they had to be able to pass each other without reacting, and they had to learn how to do a sit/stay. That's it. And of course, no jumping, pulling, biting, or aggressive behavior.

It was fun, and seeing other people struggle with their dogs gave me hope. Bella wasn't the only one with challenges, and several other puppies had just as much energy as she did. If someone could have told me at that moment that she would evolve into a mature dog able to compete in agility trials and then work as a therapy dog, I would have laughed. I couldn't see it, but I kept reminding myself that things worth doing took time. A few months later, Bella graduated from this class with flying colors, and as we neared her first birthday in January, she had begun to settle down. She knew what to expect, and except for squirrels and a few other irresistible distractions, she mostly obeyed. Even at her worst moments, she made it clear that she wanted to please us—that we were her pack.

PART II: FINDING THE RIGHT JOB

Chapter 8

SAYING GOODBYE

April 2012
Moving to Stonington, Connecticut

I 've always hated saying goodbye and was terrible at it. In third grade, I remember the last day of school and my teacher, Mrs. Armstrong, standing at the door to the classroom. She was a good teacher, but tough (no recess if you answered a question wrong, a whack on the knuckles if you misbehaved), but as I approached her, I felt my face burning as tears slid down my face. I couldn't look at her—couldn't talk—and ran from the room, out of the school, and onto the bus, hoping that no one would see me crying. I couldn't believe that she'd never be my teacher again.

I was also not very good at moving. I was a rooter—I liked to be in one place and was the kind of person who liked to know everyone in my neighborhood. In fact, Bob and I earned the title Icons of the Neighborhood. But now we were a few days away from closing on our house in Pennsylvania, where we had lived for the past twenty-four years. Our movers were coming to help us pack. We had reservations at a local hotel that took pets for our last few nights, as there would be no place to sleep and no way to cook once everything was in boxes.

I was in hyper mode as the team of packers worked through the house—I took picture hooks out of the walls, found spackle to fill the holes, ran from one room to another, answered the movers' questions, gave directions, and thoroughly exhausted myself. It felt so strange to be in what was still "our house," knowing it soon wouldn't be, and having everything in such turmoil. I had to keep Bella and Henry in one room so they were not underfoot, and Bella was trembling—she didn't like the noise and confusion. I took her on several walks to calm her down, and for the last time she got to hang out with her favorite friends: Brandon, Cooper, and Lela.

I was on autopilot and willed myself not to cry. We made it through the packing and loading of the moving truck the next day and the farewell parties. As I hugged my best friends, I told myself that I'd see them again and that we weren't really saying goodbye. It was really strange to be staying at a hotel in our own town, but the animals adjusted and before we knew it, we were at the closing Monday morning. Henry was in his travel case, Bella had been fed and walked, and we were hoping to be on the road to Connecticut by mid-morning. They were both in the car and we had left several windows open since it was a cool, end-of-April day.

An hour into the meeting, there was a snag with the buyer's check. I got Bella and brought her into the room, but I was worried about Henry, as we had a four-and-a-half hour drive in front of us and he had no access to food, water, or a litter box. At the second-hour mark, I made it clear that we had to leave, and our realtor came up with a good solution—she would deposit the check for us in our bank so that we could get going. We wished the new owners the best, thanked the rest of the team, and drove out of our wonderful town on the banks of the Delaware River. Bob had Bella in his car, and I had Henry in mine. I was more stunned than sad. We did it. We were leaving, and I had no idea what lay ahead. Thankfully, we'd already fallen in love with our small coastal town in Connecticut.

Age is a funny thing. Neither Bob nor I felt old, but we were sixty-three and sixty-five as we settled into our new home. Bella was five and Henry was eight. But in the months—really more like years—of planning for this move, we realized we wanted to do it before we were too old and the physical demands of moving became too difficult. We wanted to move while we could still make friends and find important ways to be part of our new community. We bought the house in Connecticut almost four years ago and had spent every moment there that we could—vacations, holidays, as many days as we could take off of work, Bella and Henry both making the trek back and forth with us. But now Bob had just retired, and I was in transition (the best euphemism for being laid off)—wanting to work part time, but not able to imagine my life without teaching or counseling. Bella had four months of experience as a therapy dog, so once we had a few clear paths between the endless (eighty-eight to be precise) boxes, I called our new vet to ask if he knew anyone involved in pet therapy work. He told me he did and that he was having dinner with Kat that week and would give her my contact information.

Here in Southeastern Connecticut, I was lucky to have Kat and her two Australian Shepherds, Boo and Wren, to show us around. They had been doing this for a while. In fact, several years ago Kat was one of the founders of the hospital pet therapy program. By the following week, she and I connected and she had invited us to join them for a bite-prevention program in Groton, two towns over.

"What exactly is that?" I asked her.

"The local hospital launched this program to prevent children from getting bitten by dogs. It's really good—the kids watch a video about how to interact safely with dogs, and then we bring in a few therapy dogs so they can practice what they've just learned."

Kat and I agreed to meet at the Park 'n Ride near the highway, and as she had a van, she drove us to the school in Groton. Her dogs were in crates in the back of the van, which was perfect for Bella, as she could sniff them and get used to them on her own terms.

Kat parked in the shade, left Boo in the van in her crate with plenty of water, and with Wren and Bella we entered the school and went down the hall to one of the kindergarten rooms. When we walked into the room, all the children turned to see the dogs, excited by this unfamiliar event. The teacher managed to keep them sitting on the floor, and then introduced the woman from the hospital who showed the video. There must have been fifty children in the room. I was wondering how Bella would do with so much stimulation. Before the children were allowed to pat the dogs, we were asked to tell them a little bit about their history and what they do.

Kat went first and told them about Australian Shepherds and how smart they were. Wren did a few tricks, the best being lying down on his side and closing his eyes when Kat said, "Time for bed." Now it was our turn.

"This is Bella, and she was born in Puerto Rico. She didn't have a home and was living on the beach with a lot of other dogs. But a woman found her, took her into her home, and a little while later, Bella was flown to an animal shelter in New Jersey. We adopted her when she was about four months old and now she's five years old."

"Me too!" said several kids.

Bella sat quietly by my side, looking around the room.

"She just started working as a therapy dog so she's a beginner. We both are. One thing she doesn't like is to be patted on the head, so when it's your turn to say hello, please pat her on the back. She likes that.

"Bella is a little shy and there are still a lot of things she's afraid of. But what's neat is that she learned how to be a therapy dog— how to be a dog that visits sick people in the hospital. And just like me, she likes having that job. It makes her feel good."

The hospital woman made a few more comments and then it was time for us to work the crowd. My grandchildren—Molly and her two siblings, William and Lucy—were six, four, and two at the time. Bella was good with them, so I was hopeful that this would all work out. Slowly we walked through the sea of children, and Bella decided that what most of them needed was a good lick on the face. She ducked her head and, before they could turn away, planted nice, wet kisses on their faces. They screamed— mostly with pleasure. Just like with the Girl Scouts, these were her puppies.

After that, the children stood up in two lines—one for Bella and one for Wren. They had to first say, "May I pet your dog?" Once we said yes, they could do it. Bella didn't like this routine, so to keep her from backing up and hiding behind me, I put a treat in each child's hand and let them give it to her. This worked. By the end of forty-five minutes, we were both exhausted. The teacher and the Bite-Prevention woman thanked us and the children yelled, "Goodbye, Wren! Goodbye, Bella!"

"She did really well," Kat said, as we went back down the hall and exited the school.

Her feedback meant a lot to me, as she was an evaluator of therapy dogs—the one who decided if they got certified.

"That was intense," I said, watching Bella prance down the school hall next to Wren.

Once outside, we chatted a while as the dogs sniffed around in the grass and did their business. We arranged to visit the local hospital together once I got all the paperwork done. We had successfully made it through our first assignment in Connecticut. It felt really good and I liked Kat. She was down-to-earth and very good with her dogs. And it was the first thing I'd done in our new community that made me feel as though I belonged there. That made this place seem permanent—and it was a wonderful change from unpacking boxes.

🐾 🐾

In those early weeks, I was still in shock, asking myself many times a day: "Do we really live here? Don't we have to go back to Pennsylvania?" and "How am going to find a job?" I found another dog therapy team: Deb and her lab, Shelby. Deb attended my church and was introduced to me by a friend who had moved from Yardley to Stonington several years before we did. Deb gave me the name and number of the volunteer coordinator at a local rehab facility, The Starfish Home, where she and Shelby volunteered every Wednesday. I called Starfish and sent in Bella's paperwork.

On Wednesday, June 6, we met Deb in the Starfish parking lot in Mystic. Bella was not sure she liked Shelby, a large, calm lab, also a rescue. Her hair rose and she let out a low growl. I kept myself between the two dogs and asked Deb about Shelby. She was found in Tennessee—a stray—and Deb adopted her at what her vet thought was about age two—which turned out to be more like four. We kept them away from each other as we walked around the parking lot, although Shelby was so laid back it was hard to imagine that anything could upset her.

I was nervous about going inside since I had almost no experience with nursing homes. My first impression was that these institutions were housing for people who were waiting to die, and that most of the residents wouldn't know a dog from a chair. I told myself this was simply an experiment and if we didn't like it, we wouldn't return.

Bella sniffed the grass and seemed to forget about Shelby, but I told Deb (like the parent of a gifted but difficult child), "Bella doesn't do well with new dogs. I think she's afraid."

"Don't worry about it," said Deb. "They'll get used to each other. Let's go in."

We followed them and watched as she pressed a red button that unlocked the front door. We entered a cheerful entryway with a large sitting room on the left, and another straight ahead. They were empty. We walked past these and went down a long hallway. I smelled some kind of cleaning chemical and noticed how the sun shone through the windows that lined the hall. *Not so bad*, I told myself. Plants sat on the sills—some fake, some real. A purple orchid.

Deb and Shelby had been coming here for several months, and they were both pros. I quickly learned that Deb was fearless. She poked her head into a room and said in a loud voice (because almost always the TV was on and many residents were hard of hearing), "Would you like a visit from the dogs?"

Bella and I hung back like shy children as Deb strode into each room announcing, "This is Shelby. And we have new friends today—Jean, and her dog, Bella." Shelby was perfect for this work. She loved everyone and nothing upset her.

We were in Jane and Mary's room. Shelby sat beside Jane's chair and let her head be scratched and patted while Bella pranced nervously around. "Are they sisters?" asked Mary.

"No," I told her, a tiny woman in her arm chair. "They just met today."

"Oh, but they look alike."

"You're right—they're both part lab."

"But," added Deb, "Shelby is the big one. She loves to eat!"

I'm guessing Shelby weighed more than ninety pounds, while Bella, with her dominant Whippet genes, was forty. They could be sisters. Their coats were almost the same color—Shelby's was a bit curlier and redder, but they both had brown noses with pink spots, and that lab sweetness to their faces. After a few minutes, Deb told them that we'd be back next week. I had been breathing through my mouth, as the smells in the room were strong—a mixture of human waste, chemicals, and who knows what. I wondered what Bella made of them. I wondered what they told her about the residents. As we worked our way day down the hall, most of the rooms were fine, but a few made me gag. This was more challenging than the hospital.

I watched Deb and Shelby, so comfortable, so unafraid, and noticed how their presence made the faces of the residents light up. This was clearly the highlight of their week. I coaxed Bella with treats and got her close enough so the residents could pet her. She seemed to instantly like some people, and others she was not so sure about. Just as we were about to leave a common room where we'd visited with four or five residents, Bella jumped up on the lap of a large man in sweat pants seated in a recliner.

"Oh," he said, clearly pleased that this creamy white dog had landed in his lap.

"I'm so sorry," I said. "She wasn't supposed to do that."

At least Chuck—this man—wasn't frail and Bella hadn't disconnected any tubes. Before I could get her to jump down though, I saw how his face had softened and that he was slowly running his fingers down the length of her back. He couldn't talk, but he was looking at Bella, holding her. He was no longer alone. She sat still, somehow knowing her place and that this was what she was there for. The pain and frustration of whatever ailed him evaporated in this unlikely connection.

Deb had her mouth open, clearly as stunned as I was. "Isn't she something?" she said.

I nodded and told Chuck that we looked forward to seeing him again next week. He looked at me as if I was speaking a strange language, but nodded, the brightness in his face fading. I put my arms around Bella and lifted her carefully off his lap.

Once we were back out in the hall, we laughed. "Oh, my God," I said, "I was afraid she'd hurt him."

Deb told me not to worry about it and then added, "If Shelby did that, his legs would be paralyzed for life!"

The rest of our first visit was uneventful. We followed Deb and Shelby—the very best teachers—and paid very close attention. That was all we needed to do.

Chapter 9

ONE STEP FORWARD AND FIFTEEN BACK

Spring 2008
Yardley, Pennsylvania

The title of this chapter was one of my mother's favorite expressions articulating how difficult progress—true progress—could be. When she said it, I always imagined a person walking up a steep hill, taking one step up and fifteen back, and wondered where on earth they'd end up. As a child I was very good at walking backward so I didn't see this as a bad thing— just more proof of the odd things grownups expected.

But in 2008, as Bella neared her first birthday, she was still wild, and I was envious of my friend Kim whose dog, Lela (a Vizsla), could be let off-leash. When we took a hike on a nearby trail, Kim opened the car door and Lela jumped out and stayed close to her. And deep in the woods she let her run, knowing that when she called, Lela would return. This was both inspiring and discouraging; it didn't seem possible that Bella could ever be trusted, but I longed to see her run flat out, her Whippet speed making her a white blur. I often said, as she dragged me down the street on our walks, "She was born to run."

Cathy and Kim, who were neighbors and good friends, reminded me that this would take time, and even at her worst moments, when she ate goose poop and didn't heel, I knew she wanted to please us. She had a sweetness and tenderness that were undeniable. She loved to have her body plastered up against mine or Bob's, her warmth, her muscular body, slowing us down and comforting us. When she was asleep and we'd pet her head and play with her soft ears, she'd roll over to expose her black and pink belly.

When I thought about it carefully, Angus had his moments too; sniffing endlessly under a bush, racing around like a banshee after a bath, and once pooping all over the living room rug when we took a walk in the neighborhood without him. I knew I had to get my expectations in line with what was possible, not with what I wanted—not with my timetable. So in a way, we were teaching each other: I worked to have her obey basic commands, and she let me know what she could and couldn't do. It was like trying to domesticate a very fast two-year-old child with sharp teeth and an insatiable passion for going after the neighborhood cats.

My vet had a surprising idea when I told him how frustrated I was. He said, "She's a perfect agility dog. She's fast and can turn on a dime."

"What's that?" I asked him.

He then explained that agility training involved jumping, going through tunnels (made of fabric), see-saws, weave poles, and a number of other obstacles that dogs competed in during timed trials.

"Some dogs," he added, "are a lot happier and easier to train if they have a job. I suspect Bella is one of these."

"Who offers agility around here?" I asked. He told me about a local dog club and suggested I look them up online. I found out they met in a barn nearby and offered classes for beginners as well as for dogs who were already competing. A few weeks later, I signed us up for the beginner class and tried to get Cathy and Kim to do it with me, but they weren't sure they were interested. So on a cold night in early March, Bob and I found the barn, walked Bella around outside for a few minutes, and entered a small room that served as a waiting area while the previous class went through their paces in the large, indoor horse ring.

Bella was not happy to be this close to other dogs she didn't know, but I kept her on a short leash and told her "Leave it!" when her hair rose like some prehistoric monster. Just like an embarrassed parent, I wanted to tell everyone nearby that she was afraid of other dogs and not really aggressive, but I kept my mouth shut. Finally, the other class left and we were asked to enter the ring and walk our dogs around the perimeter without using any of the equipment.

Bella quickly discovered that manure was a delicacy, but other than that, she did a good job. After about ten minutes, the two instructors, Gail and Tina, asked us to line up. There were about twelve dogs in the class and they explained that there was zero tolerance for any type of aggression. I was eyeing a huge, unneutered Rhodesian Ridgeback and hoped that he stayed clear of both Bella and me. His owner, a woman about my age, had no control over this huge dog and laughed when he jumped up on her, nearly knocking her over.

"You will be using your leash for a long time," announced Gail, "as we can't have dogs who aren't under control running around the barn. But eventually, as you saw in the last class, each dog will have a chance to run the course off-leash following your commands." Then she looked at Bob and me and said, "Only one of you can do this. It's fine if the other wants to observe, but a deep bond is established between a dog and his trainer in this work and it isn't effective to switch back and forth."

Bob quickly told me it was fine if I was the one to do the training since it was my idea.

"You sure?" I asked him.

"You care about this more than I do—go ahead."

I thanked him and took hold of her leash. As I looked around the barn, I thought to myself—no way. There was no way Bella was ever going to be able to do this. We were told to have consistent commands for each piece of equipment and I picked *over* for the jumps, *teeter* for the see-saw, *walk-it* for the dog walk (a raised plank that's about shoulder height), *tunnel* for the tunnel, *weave* for the weave poles, and *frame* for the huge A-frame that the dogs had to run up and down, stopping just before the ground. It was daunting but fun, and like any classroom, I learned as much from the other "students" as from the instructors. They demonstrated a skill with one of their dogs (of course, off-leash and well trained), and then, one at a time, we had to give the command and hope our dogs got it.

We were given homework, so each day I practiced with Bella in the house. I'd say "right here" and she had to come, or "stay," or "go left, go right" so that she learned direction, as well as the all-important "leave it" and "wait" (the command for the bottom of the A-frame where dogs had to stop with their two back paws on the frame and the front two on the ground). I didn't have any equipment, but practiced *wait* on the stairs, and up we went together. She had to stay at the top until I called her and then had to stop on the bottom step until I gave her the release word, *okay*.

There were treats involved—lots of treats. I become a frequent buyer at Trader Joe's because they had Charlie Bears—small, dry liver treats that fit nicely in the pocket and didn't smell. I had to carefully check all my pants before doing the laundry since I had treats every-where, and soon the neighborhood dogs knew it, too, and I couldn't walk Bella without stopping to give one to each of them.

Bob watched us with a detached look of amusement on his face—an expression mixed with a healthy dose of skepticism. Bella was smart—we both know that—but like me, she had her own stubborn ideas about how things should be done. Manure trumped a command and she was still jumpy around the other dogs, which gave new meaning to the word *unpredictable*.

As we celebrated her one-year anniversary with us in May, and the weather was warm, I really enjoyed the classes in the barn minus the frustration. We were now allowed to do one obstacle with the dog's leash attached but not holding on to it. Bella took this as an invitation to dash to the best pile of manure or run in the opposite direction.

"Get her attention!" yelled Gail.

I screamed, "Right here! Bella, right here!" and nothing happened. She was having a ball and was oblivious. Gail grabbed her leash, made her sit, and put her hands on both sides of Bella's face, grabbing her skin.

"Here!" she yelled.

Bella stood there like a teenager; confused, bored, and really not that interested.

Gail handed me the leash. "You need to practice the basic commands."

I do, I thought. *Every day*. I didn't say anything and took the leash, wishing at that moment that Bella was the Portuguese Water Dog in the class who was calm, attentive, and just got it. After class, I asked Gail if I could ask her a question. She looked tired but nodded.

"What about a shock collar? Something that would help her learn?"

"Are you kidding?" Gail looked at me as if I just suggested that Bella have her legs cut off. "We don't do that. You've got to work with this dog, meet her where she is, and with lots of repetition, she'll get it."

My thought? Sure, by that time she'll be an old dog and neither of us will be able to run around the barn let alone compete in agility trials.

"Thanks," I muttered, and left the barn.

Once outside I told her "Good girl" because, despite my frustration, I knew she was. I gave her as long as she liked to sniff the grass and enjoy the warm, moist air of spring. There were horses out in the pasture and a donkey brayed. I opened the back car door, told her "up," and drove home. I wasn't going to give up just because it was difficult. We had embarked on an adventure and couldn't turn back now. And besides, a competitive and stubborn part of me wanted to show the owners of the fancy designer dogs that an all-American mutt could do just as fine a job as their purebreds could—I was convinced of it.

Chapter 10

BEVERLY

May–July 2012
Stonington, Connecticut

We were back at The Starfish Home with Deb and Shelby, and Bella had decided that Shelby was not a threat. She gently licked her lips; a loving sign of submission. Deb and I laughed. "She's a sweetheart, isn't she?" Deb asked.

I wanted to say yes, but all I could think of was how she still liked to eat goose poop, and despite a lot of training, was still headstrong and unpredictable. But Deb was right—Bella was sweet, and her face was vulnerable with those soft brown eyes making her look like a puppy.

About halfway through the facility, we went into Karen and Beverly's room. I still wasn't used to being in a rehab facility— the smells were sometimes staggering and the vacant looks and slumped bodies made me want to run. But I had two really good guides: Deb and Shelby, who were always so relaxed and comfortable. To them, this was a stroll in the park. They sauntered into a room, always glad to see the resident, no matter what condition he or she was in. Bella and I still held back, waiting, learning, uncertain about our roles. Some of my old fears about places like this surfaced—a queasy feeling, a *get me out of here* and *I hope to never be in a place like this.*

Karen was a talker and loved dogs. In fact, her bed was covered by more than forty stuffed animals, which included dogs, cats, skunks, and other creatures. She was in a large reclining chair near the door and she reached out hungrily to Shelby while looking at Bella.

"Who's this?" she asked.

"This is Bella and Jean. They're new. They'll be coming with us most weeks."

I gave Karen a treat to give Bella and after Bella took it, Karen said, "More."

So we repeated this process a few times. Out of the corner of my eye, I saw her roommate—a woman I would guess was in her early eighties, holding two dolls to her chest. She was rocking slowly back and forth. I knew from the name plate outside the room that this was Beverly, and Deb had mentioned that she was not responsive.

As I got Bella away from Karen, I took a step toward Beverley and was hit by a look from her that stopped me dead in my tracks. Her scowl said: *I am somewhere terrible, I can't get out, and I hate you.*

I quickly turned back to Karen and listened to the same story about how she was sprayed by a skunk as a young woman, and then she said, "Why won't you give me treats to give the dog?" As she had already given both of them lots of treats, I turned to Deb.

"Just one more, Karen," she said, and we left the room.

Deb whispered to me once we were out in the hall, "You think she's fine, but then she doesn't remember what's happened two minutes ago."

I nodded and said, "Beverly is scary. Did you see that look on her face?"

"Just off in her own world, I guess," said Deb, cheerfully entering the next room.

Before we returned to The Starfish Home the next week, I thought about Beverly, wondering if there was a way to break through to her—a way to reach her. I gave myself a pep talk: I would not be afraid. "It's okay to fail," I told myself, "but it's not okay to judge her based on how she looks." I didn't know what it was about her that made me want to try—that pulled me toward her despite my fear. Bella had no such anxiety and would go anywhere as long we were together and treats were part of the deal.

The following week, Beverly was sitting in a chair in the hallway, again clutching the two dolls. I stopped beside her while Deb was in their room with Karen, and said, "Such nice babies. You've got two babies."

I got the same stare but noticed that she was jiggling them up and down. "You're doing a good job," I told her, then joined Deb and Shelby and continued on down the hallway. As we passed her again on our way to another wing, I said, "See you next week, Beverly," and again I was met with the hollow eyes and a dark look.

I followed Deb into a room with two men. The first, Chuck, was a big guy in sweat pants, who looked like a former football player. He was the one Bella had jumped up on a few weeks earlier. Deb told me he loved dogs and often stroked the air beside him as if his own dog were there. He couldn't talk but his face lit up when he saw Bella and Shelby. After Shelby had stood patiently by his side while he ruffled her fur, I got Bella next to him and asked if he'd like to give her a treat. No response, so I put a small treat in his hand. In one swift motion, he put it in his mouth.

"Oh, no!" I said, and his wife, who was sitting in a chair on the other side of the bed, forced his jaw open and snagged the treat with her finger.

"That's not for you!" she shouted. "It's for the dog!"

Chuck didn't respond, but looked off in the distance, off into a world that only he could see.

I apologized to his wife, and before we left, he turned his attention back to the dogs and stroked Bella. He didn't smile, but the sadness loosened at the edges of his broad face.

When Deb and I got outside in the parking lot, letting the dogs wander around on the grass, we talked about Chuck. "I guess the treats won't kill him," I told her. "They're liver. Might even be organic."

"Yuck!" she said, and we both laughed and agreed to meet in the parking lot at the same time the next week.

The third time I met Beverly, she was in her room, again sitting on the side of her bed with her babies. I gave her a few moments to get used to me and then knelt down on the floor in front of her. I could see her looking at Bella.

"Would you like to give her a treat?" I asked. Nothing. "She's my baby," I added, kissing Bella's head and giving her a treat.

Beverly's look changed from scary to whatever the first cousin of curiosity is, so I decided to be brave and gently took one of her hands, put a treat on her palm, and lowered her hand so that Bella could reach it. As Bella's tongue touched her palm, Beverley's eyebrows shot up. I let go of her hand and clapped my hands. "You did it!" I told her, and she smiled. She smiled and it was like the sun came out from behind a dark cloud. It was a miracle. There was mischief and joy for one tiny moment. And then, without dropping the babies, she clapped, too. Right at that precise moment—we became friends.

At first we tried to pretend that all residents were equal and that we didn't have favorites, but it wasn't true. My relationship with Beverly evolved as Deb's did with Wendy, a woman in her forties with Down's syndrome. Wendy couldn't really talk, but the minute she saw Deb and Shelby (and we found out she had a lab as a child), she threw her arms open wide waiting for a hug. Deb leaned down and put her arms around her, saying to Wendy, "I'm so glad to see you." Wendy wouldn't let go. The aide, a young college girl, watched and smiled, and after a bit Wendy loosened her hold and Deb straightened up. "You look beautiful today, Wendy," said Deb. "I really like your purple shirt."

Wendy smiled. Bella didn't mind missing out on this visit, as I think she was a little afraid of Wendy—or maybe the wheelchair scared her.

Deb kept talking to Wendy, never taking her hand off her arm. Never letting Wendy's erratic movements put her off. Shelby was right there by her side, basking in Wendy's attention, never pulling back as Wendy's hand flew past her face, once getting hold of her nose. Somehow she seemed to know that this was the best Wendy could do. I was learning a lot about patience and tolerance from this dog.

When it was time to go, Deb told Wendy, "See you next week, okay?"

Wendy flung her head to one side and watched Shelby. She loved this dog. As we continued down the hallway, Deb said to me, "Isn't it funny how certain residents bond with us? You have your Beverly and I have Wendy."

Beverly now seemed to be waiting for me, perhaps knowing I'd spend time with her and admire her babies. Of course, there were good days and bad days. Days she buried herself under a blanket on her bed and wouldn't come out. Days when nothing got through the dull stare. But one visit, I found her seated in a chair at one of the dining room tables eating a bag of potato chips. I was shocked, as I'd never seen her eat and didn't know she could feed herself. An aide told me she was hungry, but how did she know? The dolls lay in her lap as she licked the salt off her fingers. Another week, the dolls had been replaced by a fluffy pink rabbit.

"Oh, Beverly," I said. "Look what you have."

She glanced up at me and back down at the rabbit.

"So pretty," I added, not knowing if I should call the rabbit a baby or a rabbit. Not knowing what she saw.

"Bella would like that." I didn't tell her that Bella was a master of destruction and could rip that bunny into pieces in less than two minutes. Bella seemed to know that she wasn't needed most of the time when I was with Beverly and sat quietly to one side.

"Soft," I added, patting the rabbit.

Beverly had a shy look on her face, and I caught a glimpse of her as a girl.

"Want to me sing to it?"

Her eyebrows shot up, a quick alert moment.

"Rock a-bye baby on the tree top," I sang. I sang the whole song, remembering my two children as infants, maybe even remembering my own mother singing to me. It was a strange lullaby with destruction at the end. Just like Beverly. No one else heard us in our moment together. We focused our attention on the pink bunny, and in that way told each other we'd be there for each other. Just like good friends.

As always, Deb and I debriefed in the parking lot, praising our dogs for their amazing work. Their presence seemed effortless, but I knew by the long nap Bella took after we got home that it wasn't. This was work—hard work—being surrounded by strange smells and noises, machinery, carts being pushed down the hallways, and each room, each patient, different. There was no slacking off.

On our next visit, Deb told the head nurse, Bonnie, that I almost always made Beverly laugh, but she didn't believe it until she watched us. One day, she followed me into Beverly's room and we went through our routine.

I patted the babies, sang to them, and then said something silly.

"Is that baby being a good girl?" I asked in a high voice.

Beverly looked up.

"You be a good baby," I said, pretending to scold the one nearest me, shaking my finger at her.

Beverly grinned.

I threw my head back and laughed, and Beverly laughed, too, her missing and black teeth making her joy even more amazing.

"That is so good," said the head nurse. "I've never seen her do that. Beverly lives pretty much in her own world."

I thought we all did, but didn't say that. I wanted to ask the nurse how long she'd been here, and if she had family who visited, but I couldn't. Therapy dog teams must always respect patients' privacy. We weren't allowed to ask questions about medical history or why someone was there or in the hospital. We visited, we left, and we kept information private. But that didn't stop us from becoming part of a place.

I always thought about Beverly on the drive home; how she was that day, what she liked, what I could try on the next visit. Beverly now took to bringing the babies up to her face and kissing them. I told her that they loved her, and that she was a wonderful mother. And the next moment, I made silly kissing noises and Beverly pulled the dolls away from her face and grinned at me. I realized we didn't need words. Her look, her eyes on mine, her funny smile meeting mine—were very much like teaching Bella agility—our bodies did all the talking.

Chapter 11

AN ALL-AMERICAN DOG

2009–2010
Yardley, Pennsylvania

The world of dogs, like the world of horses, is a unique universe. There are rules, standards, expectations, and sometimes judgment. As part of our agility training and to prepare for agility trials (which were still a long way off), I filled out the paperwork so that Bella was registered with the American Kennel Club, or AKC. Until recently, mixed breeds (what we used to call mutts) were not allowed to join, but eventually there was enough pressure to include them. They were labeled as "All American." So my crazy rescue from Puerto Rico was now known as an All-American dog, and I had the paperwork to prove it.

This didn't mean that the people with fancy, purebred dogs looked on her kindly, but it did mean that she could compete. It reminded me of seventh grade when the popular girls had a certain look that the rest of us envied and did our best to emulate, knowing we'd always be outside their golden circle. My competitive nature made me even more determined to prove the Sheltie and Border Collie owners wrong, despite Bella's erratic behavior in class. I might have been more of a terrier than Bella was.

What I couldn't see at the time was that I wasn't ready to devote my life to this. I didn't want to spend every weekend going to trials, and although I enjoyed the classes for the most part—as did Bella—it wasn't the center of my life. I was working, writing, and now had two grandchildren with a third on the way. Bella's work was only a piece of the puzzle—not the whole thing. A year into the classes, we still showed up every week, freezing in the unheated barn in the winter, and sweltering and swatting flies in the summer. Bella had finally begun to get it. She knew how to jump and sail over twenty-inch rails with no problem. She eventually got over her fear of the tunnel and shot through it like a bullet. Her favorite obstacle was the A-frame, which she ran up so fast, her hind legs were suspended in the air as she went over the peak and started down the other side. What I couldn't get her to do was stop with only her front paws on the ground. Over and over I said, "Wait!" and over and over she was so excited and so fast that she flew off the obstacle.

Another challenge was the weave poles—getting her to start on the correct side of the first pole and then thread her body through without missing a single one. We started with them far enough apart that it wasn't that hard, but as the poles were placed closer together, it demanded greater concentration. I ran beside Bella and with my left hand pointed to the poles, shouting "Weave!" She would get through two or three and then run out, looking very proud of herself.

"No!" I told her, bringing her back to start all over again. When she did it right, she got a treat. As our instructors liked to say, "Do *you* work for free?" And for the really challenging sequences like doing figure eights over a series of jumps, it helped to have stinky treats. Something with salmon or bacon in it. Something motivating.

We were mostly women of a certain age, in our late fifties or early sixties, except for one man, Ted, who was amazing. He and his dog were dance partners, and they glided through the course as though they'd been doing it their whole lives. I said to another woman, "I don't think Bella and I will ever be like that." And it's true—we wouldn't. Bella was more interested in adventure, in running, in doing her own thing. In these ways, she was a lot like me. Despite her limitations, I loved seeing Bella master a skill like the dog walk—the high plank that initially scared her. With enough repetition and the lure of treats, she got it, and nearly pranced with pride as I told her "Good girl."

Another woman, whose dog was too old to continue, gave me a jump so we could practice at home. With my friend, Kim, whose dog Lela was now also taking classes, we bought weave poles and shared them. I brought Bella out to the yard as often as I could, and over and over she ran through the weave poles. Cathy and Brandon also signed up, but they were in the beginner class with Kim and Lela, while Bella and I were in advanced beginners. We enjoyed talking about class and what our dogs were learning, but I was the only one crazy enough to think that Bella would someday be able to compete.

🐾 🐾

If I had thought of agility training like math class, I would have realized much sooner that a great deal of success depended on the teacher. Gail and Tina were good and knew their stuff, but as I got to know them, I saw that Gail was deeply frustrated by her own dogs (Dalmatians with as strong a wild streak as Bella), and that Tina, an animal behaviorist with five Australian Shepherds, was more interested in her dogs than the class. As we started our second year, Gail cut her schedule back. A new teacher was hired, and Tina became a participant.

Sue, our new teacher, was amazing. She knew animals, having been a horse trainer before taking on agility. She forced us to think like dogs and she made learning fun. One evening in class, it was our turn to run the course. She said to me, "Jean, you talk too much and all Bella hears is yap, yap, yap. No wonder she won't pay attention to you."

"Oh," I said, suspecting she was right, but not knowing what to do.

"Now, you and Bella are going to run this course again and you can do whatever you want with your body, but you can't say a word. Got it?"

I nodded, wondering how this was going to work. I got Bella into position on one side of a jump, held my hand up like a traffic cop while I positioned myself on the other side of the jump and halfway to the tunnel, the next obstacle. Then, I put my hand down and made a sweeping motion so that she'd go over the jump. And she did it! I pointed to the tunnel and ran like crazy to beat her to the other side. Out she came, and I gestured to the A-frame and then the teeter. She made it halfway over the teeter and bailed. I signaled her back to me and we approached it again, but this time I stayed close to her side so she wouldn't be afraid. She did it and I clapped! Two more jumps and we were done.

"That's it!" shouted Sue. "Perfect! When you practice at home, keep your mouth shut. Bella's not an easy dog, but she watches you. She loves you. Build on that."

I was so excited I couldn't stand still. "Good girl, Bella," I told her, giving her several treats. "What a good girl."

But despite moments like these, the frustrations mounted. Every week, Tina had to run each of her five dogs through the course and it took forever. Also, having been the teacher, she was clearly not one of us and always went first. When I suggested that a few other dogs have a chance to do the course after her first three ran, I got a look. She was the professional, the expert with purebred dogs, and who was I to challenge her?

What surprised me was that no one else said anything. They deferred to her and I realized it was not a battle worth fighting. But it took a lot of joy out of the class. As Bella and I advanced, more and more teams were going to the agility trials, and when a dog got a ribbon, its owner brought in goodies so we could all celebrate. That was fun but also stressful—when would it be our turn?

The paperwork for trials was daunting. Bella needed a jump-height card based on her size, so we got that and learned how to sign up for our first trial, which happened to be in our small town in Pennsylvania in June. I was a wreck, but by asking a lot of other people at the trial, I got my paperwork turned in, had Bella measured again (a necessary procedure as this was her first trial), and got to the right gate at the right time. We were given five minutes to walk the course, which reminded me of catching a subway in New York City at rush hour—people and dogs were tripping over each other.

We stood and watched the teams compete before us—some did a fantastic job, while others were as challenged as Bella and I were. I had one moment of great comfort as Gail's dog not only didn't listen to her, but jumped the fence and left the ring altogether. This was a huge no-no. Someone grabbed the dog for her but I could see that she was humiliated.

Finally, the call came: *Bella, All-American*, and we entered the ring. I gave the leash to a volunteer who put it by the end of the course and put Bella in a "stay" before the first jump. I got into position between her and the next obstacle. This particular competition allowed you the choice of how you wanted to run the course, but you had to have a certain number of points within a very limited time frame. We had no room for mistakes. I gave Bella the release command—"Okay"—and we were off.

She did really well on the first three obstacles, but as she came down the A-frame and I decided to make a sharp turn to the right to get her into the tunnel, we nearly collided with the judge. That flustered me so that when we got to the tunnel and I saw that Bella was too far to the left, I gave her a little push.

"Disqualified!" shouted the judge. And it was over. I couldn't believe it. I knew not to touch her, but the urgency of getting through the run made me forget. Rather than walk off in defeat, we ran the rest of the course and I put on her leash and left the ring.

"Good girl, Bella. Good job!" I told her, getting treats out of the bag that I had left outside the ring. (Another rule—no treats during competitions.)

I was worked up and shaking, but she had done her first trial, and I knew I'd never touch her again in a competition. We were on our way.

I rushed home, told Bob all about it, and we packed up and drove to Connecticut for a long weekend. We had bought a house there a year and a half earlier as part of our plan to retire when we were ready to stop working. It was starting to eclipse our home in Pennsylvania because we loved it so much; the smell of the ocean, the sunlight, somehow more radiant reflecting off the pine wood floors of our new house, living between a fresh water pond and the cove. Each time we left to come back to Pennsylvania, it got a bit harder. And Bella and Henry, our cat, always came too. They seemed to feel the same way we did.

I believed in rewards and in freedom. In letting a dog be a dog. So one of my goals as we moved into fall and there were fewer ticks to worry about in the woods, was to train Bella to be off-leash. To let her run, let her go where she wanted, without losing her. I started small in a large field near our house in Pennsylvania—a community lot. It bordered the pond on two sides, and the road on the other side was residential and not heavily traveled.

Because Bella was obsessed with tennis balls, I used them to keep her from running away. Once I got her to the field, I unhooked her leash and quickly threw the ball. She tore after it and ran back to me. It took her a few seconds to release the ball; she didn't entirely trust me to give it back to her. We did this over and over while I was on the lookout for other dogs, stray cats, anything that might distract her.

The upper and lower pond were connected by a narrow foot bridge. I got her to go over this and let her walk a bit more before reattaching her leash. Bob was nervous, but he saw that Bella was not trying to escape as much as she loved to run.

On a chilly Saturday, Cathy, Kim, our dogs, and I headed to the trails in a nature preserve north of us. Once we were past the parking lot, Kim let Lela loose. Brandon stayed on the leash—Cathy had no interest in finding out if he would come back. With my heart in my mouth, I let Bella off the leash and she ran after Lela and then tore off into the dense woods.

"Hey, Bella!" I shouted. "Right here." Nothing happened.

We walked another five minutes and now my heart was starting to pound and I knew that Bob would never forgive me if I lost this dog. The only comfort I had was that she was micro-chipped, but that wouldn't do any good if she was lost forever in the woods or got killed by something.

Another hiker came toward us on the trail.

"Excuse me. Have you seen a white dog—midsize?"

He shook his head.

By now I was screaming Bella's name in full panic. Lela had come back, Brandon was on his leash, and the three of us stopped to listen. We heard birds, some insects, but no thrashing or sounds of a dog.

"Let's spread out," said Kim. "Jean, you stay here, I'll go ahead, and Cathy, go back a ways. We'll find her."

I wished I could believe her. I made a promise at that moment that I would never let her off-leash again. Never.

"Bella, here girl. Come on!"

The thick woods absorbed my voice. Just as I was about to cry, I heard something—something moving in the underbrush.

I made sure my voice didn't sound angry. "Good girl. Come on."

And suddenly there she was, panting, blood streaked across her face.

"Oh, Bella. Good girl. Good girl."

I quickly attached the leash, shouted to Kim and Cathy that I'd found her, and bent down to see where she was hurt. The side of one of her ears was torn. It looked as though she'd gotten caught in brambles, but the blood had stopped. She looked worse than she was.

Cathy and Kim fussed over her, and we finished our hike. At three years old, I had thought she was ready for this—I thought she'd obey. I guess the smells and adventure of the woods and of being free were too tempting. It was a long time before I tried again.

Chapter 12

LEONARD

July–August 2012
Stonington, Connecticut

On my second visit to the hospital, Kat and her dogs couldn't come. As I signed in at the volunteer office and put on my blue smock that made me look like a Wal-Mart greeter, I learned there was a request for a therapy dog on the fourth floor. The nurses were having a hard time getting a disabled patient, Leonard, to respond.

I checked in at the nurse's station on the fourth floor and asked for Leonard's room. A nurse offered to go with me. Bella had her ears up and was staying close to my left side.

"Good girl," I told her, more to comfort myself than her.

"Leonard. Someone here to see you!" shouted the nurse. The lump in the bed didn't move.

"Look, Leonard!" she said, then turned to me and asked me to pull a chair up next to the bed so that he could see Bella.

I pointed to the chair and said "Up!" Bella, all forty pounds of lab, whippet, and terrier leapt onto the chair. She looked at the bed and something moved.

"This is Bella," I said softly. Leonard's head turned and one eye opened. The nurse watched.

His hands were twisted into each other, like the gnarled roots of an old tree.

"Would you like to pet her?" Bella stayed motionless as we waited.

The other eye opened and he clearly saw the dog.

He said something like, "Neya."

"You can give Bella a treat." I held a small, round dog treat in my hand, and as I watched, I think Leonard's eyes brightened.

"Can I put one in your hand?" No objection.

I uncurled his fingers and managed to slip a treat between his index and middle fingers as there was no way he could fully open his hand. Bella leaned forward and very gently extracted the treat. Her tongue brushed his fingers. He watched her and we stayed another ten minutes or so, just being quiet together. Before I left his room, I promised to return the following week.

The nurse said to me in the hall: "That went well."

"It did?"

"That's the best reaction we've ever gotten out of him. Please come back."

I told her I would and walked down the hall. Bella's idea of what to do after such concentration was to bite the leash and play tug-of-war.

"Not now, girlfriend. Leave it!"

Giving me a look like a sulky teenager, she did.

We visited a few other patients, always asking first, "Would you like a visit from a dog?" and I quickly learned that the friends and relatives who were visiting the patients were often as needy as the patients themselves. Sometimes more.

"Look, Mom," said a middle-aged daughter. "A dog is here to visit you. Doesn't she remind you of Goldie?"

Or a husband, keeping vigil by his wife's bed. "Thank you so much for coming in. This is the best thing I've seen all day."

I noticed that the older generation—the people in their sixties and up—had the best manners. Even in pain, they thanked me for coming in. They sensed what it took to do this work. They focused on others. Bella—who had her own ideas about what to do, how long to stay, whether or not someone could pet her on the head—didn't care about compliments. But for me, these were the equivalent of dog treats. I loved them. They affirmed what we had set out to do.

As we got used to this hospital, I learned that some visits were quick—just a hello and then we were gone—while others couldn't be rushed. It all depended on what was required. During one visit, I asked a nurse if anyone would like to see Bella and she told me to go to room 218. I knocked on the door and saw a man who looked to be about seventy sitting on a chair, his suitcase beside him. He had on navy blue pants and a T-shirt with holes in it.

"Going home today?" I asked, after introducing Bella.

"Yes, just waiting for the doctor to let me out."

Bella was not at her best, maybe because she had been besieged by the nurses as we came onto the floor, or because she missed Wren and Boo and didn't like being on her own. I let her sniff around while Jerry, the patient, and I chatted about dogs. Then, as if someone had flipped a switch, Jerry said, "My father was a coal miner. Black lung. Shoulda died at fifty-two when the doc told him it was hopeless. Son-of-a-bitch made it to seventy-nine!"

He laughed and I smiled and said, "He sure sounds tough."

Then I asked Jerry if he worked in the mines, too.

He nodded and said, "Yup, one day."

"One day?"

"That's all I lasted. I was nineteen and right out of high school. There were no other jobs in West Virginia, but when I heard that mountain crack—a terrible groaning—I turned around and ran out. Never looked back."

Bella was inching closer to a waste basket while my attention was diverted.

"Leave it!"

She obeyed.

"So what did you do?" I asked.

"Joined the army and before I knew it, I was in Korea. You don't know what cold is until you've served over there."

"Bad?" I asked.

"Blistering." And then he told me a complicated story about his sergeant who played a trick on him while he was on guard duty at night. He was on high alert since the enemy often attacked at night, and he was shivering and stomping his feet to keep them from freezing, when someone came up from behind him and grabbed him. He took his rifle butt and slammed it into the stomach of what he thought was an enemy solider. As he was about to finish off this intruder, he saw that it was his sergeant. He helped him to his feet, endured an avalanche of cuss words, and the next day faced a court martial. Instead of being in trouble, the commander told him that he should have shot his officer for playing such a stupid prank in a war zone.

He threw his head back and laughed, and I could see that he was back there and it was so real: the war, the terrible cold, and this strange twist of events.

Bella must have liked the sound of his voice; she was still and attentive. "I was lucky not to lose my toes or fingers. A lot of guys did." We talked a bit more about his service in the army, and then

I said good-bye and wished him luck getting home. As Bella and I walked down the hall, I was amazed that something I'd never given much thought to—the terrible conditions that the soldiers endured during the Korean War—was suddenly so vivid. I thought about him all the way home and thanked him for his service.

🐾 🐾

One week later, we went back to Leonard's room, but this time, when I put the chair in place next to his bed and told Bella "Up!" she wouldn't budge. I looked at her to see if something was wrong, but her clear, brown eyes looked untroubled.

"Bella, up!" I pointed to the chair, and again she refused to move. Before I could figure out what to do next, she jumped up on Lenard's bed, and in one swift motion, circled and lay down next to him.

"Oh," I said, wondering if the nurse was going to be upset. She wasn't in the room, but I had been told at orientation that it was okay for the dogs to get on the beds as long as the patient wanted it. There was no doubt, looking at Leonard, that this was exactly what he wanted.

A torrent of words escaped Leonard's mouth. Most of them I couldn't understand except the word *dog*. The nurse, who had come into the room to see how we were doing, told me she thought he had had a dog. I helped Leonard move one of his hands so that he could feel her fur. Bella was sleek; her short, white fur soft over her muscular body. She snuggled up next to him and was still while Leonard and I had a conversation of sorts. He made sounds and I nodded and smiled. But Bella didn't need words, didn't care that everything was garbled—she could feel his side along her back. She could smell him. And somehow she knew, she just knew, to simply be there.

We stayed a long time. We forgot about the other patients, as it was clear to me that this was where we belonged. I had learned something surprising—not that she was in charge, but that if I got out of the way, she would do the right thing. I smiled as I thought of myself as her chauffeur—the one who drove her to work. But that wasn't quite it either, as we worked together. We really were a team.

At the end, the nurse asked me how our visit went and then told me that no one ever came to see Leonard—not even his wife. "She came once to get him to sign over his Social Security check, and that's it."

I was stunned—how could a person be abandoned like that? I didn't get it.

"Will he go back home?" I asked her, knowing as I did that I wasn't supposed to ask about personal information.

"I don't think so. His problems are too severe."

Once out in the hallway, I gave Bella a treat and told her, "Good girl." And then, because I was so proud of her (and the hallway was empty), we played tug of war. I had to keep reminding myself that a therapy dog is still a dog. Bella's head snapped back and forth as she tugged on the leash. We both grunted with the effort and with pleasure. Before I came face-to-face with a doctor or some hospital official, I told her, "Okay, girlfriend. Leave it."

She looked up at me as if saying "really?" I nodded and she let the leash drop from her teeth. "Good girl," I told her again. I was amazed at how she "read" Leonard. How she knew just what he needed. And for several weeks, until Leonard was transferred to a nursing home, we were there every Thursday afternoon and became friends.

The boxes were mostly unpacked and we had taken endless trips to the dump to recycle the packing boxes, as well as several trips to Goodwill to give away duplicates or things we didn't need. It was a mathematical equation that I was not particularly good at: two houses down to one house. We had only so much room, and although I was not a pack rat, I couldn't part with boxes of letters and journals and my past writing projects. I told myself that I would go through them on cold winter nights. I insisted that I needed them. It took almost three years before I could even look at them.

I gave myself lectures. I'd been counseling people who had lost their jobs for almost eighteen years. I knew the routine. I'd sympathized with the emptiness, the loss, the not belonging. Career coaches called this "transition," and that made me think of labor, of giving birth—which I'd already done, twice. Transition was when all hell broke loose. When the body became a vise. When you had to submit.

I preferred control. Being naturally bossy, I wanted to run the show. I wanted a plan, answers, income, colleagues, and purpose. I wanted to be valued. I didn't want to be retired. I didn't want to be only a housewife, although I was blessed with a wonderful husband and lived in a spectacular place near the coast. I didn't want to admit that I needed help, that I was unsure of the way ahead, and that all I really wanted was to stop thinking about it. If I just got my job back, if I got hired by another outplacement firm, or by the New England office of my former company, I'd be all set. I knew how to run an effective job search, but I was like a little kid having a tantrum. I wouldn't admit it, but I was feeling sorry for myself. One day, Bob invited a college friend who lived nearby and her husband for lunch. I made a Focaccia with caramelized onions and fresh mozzarella, a salad, fresh fruit, and homemade cookies for dessert. I felt like Martha Stewart. We had cloth napkins in tropical colors, the sun was shining, and we were outside on a perfect summer day. This was home.

After lunch we took a walk to show them the neighborhood, then we sat in the library (that's what we call our family room as it has built-in bookcases), and Bob and his college buddy talked about their former friends, old professors, who did what. Her husband was like a cat sitting in the sun. He was content. He nodded. I did a lot of nodding and smiling, and then after almost an hour of this, got restless. I got up and went into the kitchen to put the dishes in the dishwasher. I grabbed Henry's comb and rejoined the group in the library and groomed Henry. That sustained me for about five minutes. I asked if anyone needed something to drink. They didn't. I realized I was invisible. I could crawl under the couch and no one would notice. And suddenly I was on the brink of tears.

I left the room again, grabbed a book and my glasses, and went back out to the patio. But I couldn't read. Tears slid down my face. I was pissed off—at Bob for not noticing and for not including me in the conversation—but mostly I couldn't stand not knowing what I was supposed to do. I was sixty-five years old, wanted to work, needed other people in my life, was deeply grateful for so many blessings—but I felt broken and discarded.

When I was first notified that I was losing my job back in October 2011, a colleague told me to read my own book, *Eliminated! Now What?* I had laughed then and told her that was great advice. Writing about it and counseling others was not the same. I could sympathize with my clients, offer helpful advice, but I hadn't been the one thrown under the bus. Even as I felt sorry for myself, I knew that I needed a change, that my world had become too small, too predictable. This made me smile, for there certainly wasn't anything routine about my life now.

Bob came out onto the patio. "What are you doing?"

I couldn't answer. He saw my face, saw the sadness, and said, "Come inside. We'll talk later."

I could tell he was upset with me, but I couldn't help it.

I rejoined our company and acted as if everything was fine. They were tentative with me now—I was clearly a wild card. A loose cannon. I did my best, but I didn't really care. For that moment, this was who I was.

Chapter 13

TIME TO WALK AWAY

Fall–Winter 2010
Yardley, Pennsylvania

In what many would call "my salad days," I lived in New York City and discovered an odd phenomenon: if a subway was late and I was standing on the platform with a whole bunch of other people, the longer we waited, the more certain I became that the train would come any second. This investment, sweltering hot in the summer and frigid in the winter with winds that howled through the station, made it impossible to leave. The same thing happened initially with agility training.

Bella had advanced several levels and could be off-leash the whole time except when we were waiting our turn. Her whippet genes made her fast, and she turned on a dime, racing from a jump to the tunnel and then through the weave poles. And I got better in helping her navigate the course, anticipating the next obstacle, trying desperately to stay ahead of her. Cathy and Kim, my two best dog friends in Pennsylvania, had both dropped out after a year, but were willing to go to a trial with Bella and me in New Jersey.

The drive took more than an hour, but once there, we walked Bella, got signed in, and found out where her event would take place. We had hours to kill but it was a beautiful fall day and it was wonderful to see other dogs compete. Some were so accomplished and had clearly been doing agility for a long time. Others, like me, were beginners and were struggling to get their dogs to follow instructions where every second mattered.

We ate lunch and finally it was Bella's turn. Unlike our first trial, for this event we had to run the course as it was set up. Numbers marked each step of the way. Parts of it were pretty easy: a jump, the A-frame, the teeter. Others were more challenging, like getting your dog to turn after a jump and circle back to run through the tunnel.

My heart was pounding as Bella's name and breed were announced. I gave her a pat (the last I'd touch her until the run was over) and got her to stay while I got myself into position. Once I said "Okay," the release word that told her we were good to go, the whole thing was a blur. After the second jump, Bella went running off across the ring and flew up the A-frame, stopping at the top to look down at me, as if saying, "Where the heck are you?"

I called her, I gestured, but she was enjoying her bird's-eye view and didn't want to come down. Now I was screaming and she finally came. I got her back on course and only had three obstacles to go when she suddenly veered off after the dog walk and circled behind me. The judge blew a whistle and we were out of time. I was angry and discouraged as I walked to the exit gate, not caring if she was with me or not. I grabbed her leash, attached it to her collar, and left the ring.

Kim and Cathy were there, and I was both glad and embarrassed to see them.

"She's learning," said Cathy, the peacemaker.

"She got some of it right," added Kim, the diplomat.

"It sucked," I said, fighting back tears.

"How can she be so stubborn, so strong-willed after all the classes we've taken and all the practice? Why doesn't she obey? Why doesn't she come when I call her?"

"She's young," added Cathy. "She'll learn."

"I don't know," I told them. "She's three and a half. Maybe she isn't meant to do this."

"Don't decide now," said Kim. "You're upset. Let's go get some ice cream and get out of here."

And we did just that.

Several people asked me how she did in class the next week, but it was obvious that we failed as we had no ribbon and I didn't bring in goodies to celebrate. I nearly got into a cat fight with Tina after she insisted on running one of her dogs a second time while the rest of us waited endlessly, shifting our weight, trying to pay attention.

On the way home I asked myself: *Why are you doing this? Who says you have to have an agility dog?* I told Bob how discouraged I was and he suggested I take a break. But I couldn't do that. I either continued or I quit. Hanging on to a hope that she would do better would just be frustrating, and I was already tense and unhappy. To top it off, I was swimming upstream at work. I had been with the same company for fifteen years and loved career counseling. What I increasingly realized I didn't love was the pressure to do more with less. My client load had almost doubled, and we were swamped with rules and paperwork. To do my job half well, I had to spend hours every Sunday before the week started, editing résumés and catching up on endless emails from clients. Bob told me not to do it, that I was giving away too much of my time, but if I waited for the workweek, I was perpetually behind and in a panic.

As my daughter would say, I was a grumpy puppy. But I liked Sue, the agility teacher, so we continued with classes and I even drove an hour each way to take a few private lessons with her. I wished I could be like her. She's was so sure of herself, so good at "reading" dogs, and equally good at figuring out people. She saw where I was pushing and asking too much and where my signals to Bella weren't clear. She was good at breaking down each part of a routine into simple steps, but when it came to running next to Bella and making it happen, Bella seemed to be fighting me every step of the way.

If I were a dog, I would have to be at least half pit bull-terrier because once I got hold of something, I couldn't let go. I ignored my frustration, I ignored Bella and the good advice of Bob and my friends. I was in what I called "bulldozer mode." I would make this work if it killed me.

So we signed up for another trial and did this one on our own. Bella was amazing. She only made one mistake, running past a jump, which I easily corrected. We were flying, moving so fast from one obstacle to the next. In between I gasped, "Good girl," and down she came, off the dog walk, and we were done. I threw my hands into the air and shouted "You did it!" But as I went to get her leash, Bella headed toward the exit of the ring. "Right here, Bella," I called, and she came to me so I could attach her leash. And then I couldn't believe what I heard. The judge said in a loud voice: "Disqualified. Left the ring."

I was stunned and couldn't move. Disqualified? After an almost perfect run? And she didn't leave the ring, she only went toward the exit and then came right back. I was so close to tears that I quickly walked away, and as I waited to buy a cup of tea for my drive home, one of the volunteers came up to me and said, "You did a good job. I have to tell you, that judge is really strict and she has a thing about dogs going out of the ring."

"But she didn't," I said.

"I know," he told me. "But that's just the way she is."

I thanked him for telling me, got my tea, and headed outdoors. As I gave Bella time to sniff around on the grass, I keep replaying what happened. Disqualified? The judge had taken what took years of practice and had thrown it out. She didn't see the way Bella sailed over the jumps or shot through the tunnel. She didn't see how she overcame her fear and pranced over the teeter. She didn't understand that this dog, who was lucky to be alive, who came from a horrible place, had grown in trust and skill and had done a fantastic job.

I wanted to kick something. I talked to myself, repeatedly dropped the f-bomb, but then I looked down at my dog, my three-year-old bundle of energy, and took a moment to give her credit. She had come such a long way.

I gave her a drink of water, got in the car, and called Bob on my cell phone.

"Almost did it," I told him, explaining what happened.

"Good for you," he told me. "I'm sorry the judge threw you out. Come home and we'll talk about it."

I took a deep breath, started the car, and turned around to make sure Bella was okay. She was sound asleep on the back seat with her tail over her nose. I found an oldies station on the radio and turned the volume up high. Nothing like singing rock and roll when you're down in the dumps.

When we returned to class the following week, Tina wanted to know how we did.

"Really well," I told her, "but the judge thought Bella left the ring so she was disqualified."

I got a smug look from her. Her dogs wouldn't do that. I wasn't past caring, but something had shifted. I saw the work we'd done here as excellent training. Bella and I were a team. We "read" each other. Because the instructors and most people in the class were focused on the trials, I was too. But it was a choice, and right now I was choosing not to put us through that. In the short, cold days of December, we finished up the few classes left in the session and thanked Gail and Tina for their help. We were done. I didn't need ribbons to know that Bella was a wonderful dog.

PART III: SIT, STAY, PAWS UP

Chapter 14

NAVIGATING THROUGH
A HOSPITAL

Summer 2012
Stonington, Connecticut

When we entered unknown territory, it was good to have a guide. Kat Bishop knew the dog world. She was an experienced handler of therapy dogs, an evaluator, and connected in our community in Connecticut. It was encouraging to me that her dogs, like Bella, were a work in progress. Boo had a strange habit of breaking into a high-pitched howl without warning. We had finished our visit and were standing near the elevators on the fourth floor of the hospital, waiting to go down to the main floor, and opposite us, exiting another bank of elevators, we saw a woman on a gurney being pushed by a young volunteer.

She must have just had surgery as she looked half-asleep and didn't notice the dogs. But when Boo let out one of her electrifying howls, she lifted up off the gurney and almost screamed. Kat was mortified.

"Oh, I'm so sorry," she said, as the woman was wheeled past us. "I didn't mean to scare you."

Boo looked very pleased with herself.

"No, Boo, no!" Kat told her.

When we got into the elevator and there was no one else inside, she told me: "I don't think this dog is going to make it."

"Because of the howl?" I asked.

"Not just that. I don't think she's suited for it."

I thought to myself, if Boo wasn't suited for therapy work, then Bella wasn't either, as she still backed away from people and was head-shy. And Boo, like Bella, radiated sweetness.

"Maybe she needs more time," I said, always the optimist, always rooting for the dog.

"I think I'll work with Wren instead. At least she doesn't make the patients levitate."

We had a good laugh as we walked down to the Community Cancer Center. Kat didn't want to go there—wasn't sure why—but I had promised my best friend that Bella and I would always stop by there as a way of supporting her fight against breast cancer, though she was being treated in a different hospital out of state. I'd done it in her honor in Pennsylvania and I'd continue to do it here. Kat and Boo hung out in the waiting room while we found the infusion room. The nurse at the front desk told me where to go and thanked me for bringing Bella in. "We never get dogs here," she told me.

The nurses in the infusion room were startled and not sure at first why there was a dog there. "This is Bella," I told them, "and she's a therapy dog. Is it all right if she visits the patients who would like to see her?"

I held up Bella's badge, which I wore on a lanyard around my neck. "She visited the infusion room back in our hospital in Pennsylvania and did a great job."

They nodded and I asked who would like to see her. A man who looked to be in his early seventies waved at me. "Bring her over," he said, "I love dogs." I'd been reinforcing a new command for Bella—*paws up*—because in the infusion room patients were seated in large recliners and couldn't reach her unless she got closer. I asked this gentleman if Bella could put her paws up on the side of his chair.

"Heck yes!" he said. "She can sit in my lap if she wants to."

That was not Bella's idea of a good time, but she would take treats from his hand, and when distracted, would let him pet her. He wanted to know about Bella so I told him her story.

"Aren't you a good girl?" he asked, and I saw that the patients on either side of him were listening.

"Yes, she is, most of the time," I answered, figuring it was better not to tell him that she didn't like a lot of other dogs, and could chew her way through anything.

"Well, that's all you can ask, isn't it?"

He looked at me and smiled, and I felt as if I were standing in bright sunlight. He had the most amazing blue eyes that sparkled and were full of life. I found out his name was Jim and after we saw him for several weeks in a row, he asked if he could tell me a story.

"Sure thing." Bella was tired, as this was always the end of our visit, and she sat down next to me.

"When I was a young man, I lived in farm country and worked on the family farm. It was hard work and there wasn't much time for socializing. But one day I had to go to the neighbor's house to see if we could borrow a piece of their equipment, an attachment for the tractor. As I was driving our tractor down the road, I saw a girl on a horse riding bareback in the field next to the road. She had beautiful long, red hair and was galloping."

"I stopped the tractor and watched. She and the horse seemed like one thing, turning this way and that, skimming over the grass. And right at that moment, do you know what I decided?"

I shook my head.

"That she would be my wife."

He looked at me to see if I believed him. I did.

"Course I had to meet her and I came to find out that she was only fifteen, but I had time. So we got to know each other and by the time she was eighteen, we were husband and wife."

"Wow," I said. "That's a beautiful story."

"But she died last year."

I saw a shadow fall over his eyes as if someone had turned the lights out. But in the next moment, his sparkle was back.

"Wasn't I lucky to have someone like that for all those years?"

"Yes," I told him. "You really were." And I was thinking she was lucky to have him, too.

"She was the best," he said quietly, slightly shaking his head as if her loss was still unfathomable.

As I walked out of the hospital, I thought of my husband, Bob, and how good it's been to be married to him. We were coming up on our thirty-first wedding anniversary. All the way home, as Bella slept peacefully on the back seat, I thought about Jim and his wife and realized that, as he told me his story, we hadn't been in the Cancer Center, and he hadn't been a patient. Instead, he was a young man on a tractor, seeing a beautiful girl gallop across a field on her horse.

Hospitals are like foreign countries—you have to learn how to get around and figure out the rules and culture. Therapy dogs were allowed in most areas of the hospital but not in the maternity ward or surgical areas. They were allowed in the Emergency Room waiting area but I didn't go there—I thought it was too tense, and I wasn't sure it was the right place for a dog. Or for Bella.

We rarely received a request, so when Bella and I were at Lawrence and Memorial Hospital by ourselves, we signed in and took the elevator up to one of the middle floors and then followed a winding set of corridors to get to a nurse's station. I introduced Bella and asked if they knew of any patient who would like a visit. Sometimes the response was immediate: "Oh, yes. Please see Room 405—the patient in the bed by the window. She loves dogs." And other times it was "Just ask."

We avoided rooms where there was a lot going on: a doctor examining a patient, or the nutritionist or physical therapist at work. But family members often saw Bella as we walked by and asked us to come in. Bella and I always focused on the patient even if he or she was not responsive, as I saw this as our primary job. So while helping Bella past the visitors, we got as close to the bed as we could and then I asked if they'd like her to put her paws up.

We were in the room of an elderly woman who was curled up on her side. Her daughter, who looked to be close to my age, was sitting in a chair next to the bed. "Look, Mom. A dog is here to visit you."

Nothing. No reaction.

"Can I bring her closer?" I asked.

"Sure," said the daughter, moving her chair back.

"Come, Bella," I said softly, and she approached the bed. "This is Bella and she's come to see you."

One eye opened.

"Would you like to pet her?"

The other eye opened and there was an imperceptible nod.

Very carefully I got Bella to put her front paws up on the edge of the bed and the woman lifted her hand and touched Bella's neck.

"Oh," she said, and smiled.

That was it.

"Good girl," I said to Bella as she put her paws back down on the floor.

"That was beautiful," said the daughter. "She hasn't responded to anything in a long time. Thank you."

"You are very welcome," I said, and we left the room, me wondering what this patient saw when she looked at Bella. Was she far away, as if in a cocoon, and then there were those brown eyes with the short white lashes, a face full of sweetness with freckles on her nose? Was that like a spirit, like wind blowing through the room?

When my mother was dying, my brother asked her what it was like and she said softly, "Drifting. Just like drifting."

She wasn't in pain, she knew we were there, and as the night progressed, as my brother and sister and I took turns taking cat naps, we sang to her—every song we could think of. Show tunes, the Beatles, Christmas carols. The room was dim and the nurses came by. They watched and listened. One or two even joined in. They told us the next morning, after she died, that it was beautiful. That it was a blessed way to go.

Back in the hallway, I cleaned my hands from one of the wall dispensers and gave Bella a treat. "Good job, girlfriend."

Like any other work or project, a lot was unremarkable about our visits. We went into rooms, had short chats, often sharing Bella's story (as it was classic *Cinderella*: Dead Dog Beach to Therapy Dog) and left. But there were moments like this last one that broke through the chatter, and busyness, and ordinary times, and I was stunned by what Bella could do. Stunned and so very proud.

Now that we were living in Connecticut, I was determined to train Bella to run off-leash and come back to me. One of our favorite hiking places was Barn Island—a huge tract of land that ran along the coast, a preserve for hunters. Since it wasn't hunting season, we hiked for about ten minutes, then unclipped her leash. She was a bullet and took off up the trail, suddenly stopping, veering off into the marsh grasses. We saw the tip of her tail appear, we heard splashing, and I ran ahead to make sure she was all right.

"Bella! Right here!"

I held my breath. I saw the look in Bob's eyes, the fear that she was lost forever, and then the splashing got closer and a brown, mud-covered dog appeared at our feet looking very pleased with herself.

"Good girl!" I said, as she hurled herself onto the grass path, rolling in ecstasy.

"Let's keep going," I told Bob, and we walked through pin oaks and moss-covered trees. A forest at the edge of the ocean.

Bella was like a yo-yo, darting off, coming back, a wild look in her eyes.

"Don't you think you should leash her?" asked Bob.

"Not yet. This is so good for her."

This was a dog in dog heaven. She was covered in mud, panting, doing exactly what she wanted. After about a mile, we took a break and sat on a large rock in the shade. Bella flopped down next to us and I gave her a few treats.

As we headed back toward the parking lot, Bella went into mach speed. It didn't seem possible after what she had done so far, but now she was running on water. She flew off a small mound of earth into the marsh, out again, up the bank to the trail, and off on the other side, never slowing down. When she got to a deep tidal pool, she swam, then flipped her body onto the sandy trail, rolling so hard that her head touched her tail. As soon as we caught up, she was off again, crashing through the woods, branches cracking, leaves flying.

"How are you going to catch her?" asked Bob.

"I don't know, but I will. She's got to get tired at some point."

"No sign of it," said Bob, looking off into the woods where it sounded as if a giant was flattening the landscape.

"Bella, right here!"

I stood still and waited, hoping she would recognize my voice and remember that she was supposed to come.

Silence. We waited. Finally, a hundred yards ahead of us, we saw her emerge from the water.

"Stay, Bella!" I commanded, and she flopped down on the ground.

We caught up, I clipped the leash to her harness, and gave her several treats, praising her profusely.

"I bet she takes a long nap," said Bob, relief written all over his face.

"After a bath," I said, smelling the brackish water and mud that coated her fur.

There was nothing as exciting as watching Bella run. She flattened her body, crouched close to the ground, and became a blur—a white streak.

I wiped her off with a towel before letting her in the car, and once she jumped up on the back seat, she was instantly asleep. This dog, this wild creature who was born to run, was anything but gradual.

Chapter 15

CANINE GOOD CITIZEN

Winter–Summer 2011
Yardley, Pennsylvania

Cathy came to my rescue. Just after the holidays, when I was missing the focus that agility training gave Bella and me, she suggested we get Bella and Brandon certified as therapy dogs.

"What would they do?" I asked, having a vague memory of reading about dogs who helped people.

"Lots of things," said Cathy. "They can go in hospitals, nursing homes, schools, the courthouse. Just about anywhere, I guess."

Cathy saw me hesitate. "They're not service dogs. It isn't that level of training. It's more relaxed. I think they make people feel good."

"You think they'd pass?" I asked, still a bit bruised from my agility experience.

"I don't know, but wouldn't it be neat to try?"

I nodded, still not sure what to say.

"Can you imagine taking Bella into a hospital? Wouldn't she be awesome?"

I had never seen a dog in a hospital, but the idea grabbed me. She would be something.

"Are you okay about finding out about it and then I'll decide?" I asked her. I was torn because I liked the idea, but felt stressed at work and wasn't sure if adding another project made sense. I found myself exhausted at the end of the day, and I didn't think it was my age, but more the frustration of always being behind. No matter how hard I tried, there were endless résumés to edit, more calls to return, more new clients to work with.

Cathy was dauntless. "Sure thing."

But I realized I missed the special time that Bella and I had in classes. It was like going dancing—just that other person and no distractions.

Before long, Cathy had done the research and found a local class that would help prepare us for the first requirement: passing the Canine Good Citizen (CGC) test. I loved this name; who wouldn't want a dog who was a good citizen? I read up on it and learned there were two parts to this: responsible pet ownership for the humans, and good behavior for the dogs. If you passed this ten-step process, you received a certificate from the American Kennel Club.

Cathy and I signed up, and on a cold, January night, she picked us up, Bella joining Brandon in the back seat.

"This should be fun," I said, intrigued by the idea that Bella could become a therapy dog.

"I worry about Brandon and other dogs," said Cathy. "You know how he is, Mr. Know-It-All."

"I think Bella is just as bad. She either loves other dogs or hates them, and there's no middle."

We entered the training facility and were told to wait in the vestibule while the previous class finished. "Please don't let your dogs bother the other dogs as they leave," said the receptionist.

Not a problem, I thought, keeping Bella on a short leash right next to me. A woman with a large boxer entered and sat opposite us. Bella's hair rose and I saw her whole body tense. The dog looked at her like she'd make a good snack.

"Leave it," I told her, the most useful and least obeyed command in our repertoire.

Cathy and I chatted and admired the other dogs, and finally Debby, our instructor, asked us to come into the training room in single file. We followed Brandon, as I knew Bella would behave behind her buddy. We were then seated in a row of chairs along one wall in a large room carpeted in electric green Astroturf. The boxer growled at the dog next to him.

Fast as lightening, Debby was on him, pushing him onto to his side, shouting "No!"

Cathy and I looked at each other and wondered what we had signed up for. When Debby saw the stunned faces of the class, she straightened up and said, "I've worked with this dog before. He has behavioral problems that we're dealing with. Don't worry about him, I've got him under control."

"Holy shit," I whispered to Cathy. Her eyebrows seemed stuck in the raised position.

The woman who owned the boxer sat there as if she'd lost her last friend. Debby walked to the center of the room and listed the rules we must follow. No this, no that, no talking, no letting your dog get too close to another dog, no yanking on the leash, and so on. But at this moment, the rules sounded okay to me. I was excited to be doing something new, something where we could be more successful than agility, so I ignored my gut feeling about this trainer and decided the class would be a good experience—which it mostly was.

At first, things got a bit better. It was fun to walk around the perimeter of the training room with Bella, and this felt easy after weave poles and teeters. Bella walked fairly well on a loose leash and followed me when we were instructed to make a U-turn and go in the opposite direction.

I avoided the boxer and watched with pride as Cathy and Brandon looked as if they'd been doing this forever. Debby lined us up in two lines facing each other. We had to approach another team (handler and dog), shake hands with the handler, and say something like "Nice to meet you." The dogs had to sit or stand quietly at our sides and couldn't interact either with the other dog or its handler.

Bella pulled and I saw her hair lifting off her back. "Sit," I told her, and she did. But as soon as I said, "Nice to meet you," she stood up, trying to get closer to the other dog. This was going to take practice. The next exercise was to let someone pet Bella. Because we were being trained along with our dogs, we had to ask: "May I pet your dog?" and as I said yes, I mumbled, "She's a bit head-shy but likes to be touched on her neck or back." I hope this wasn't cheating.

Debby came up to Bella to demonstrate for the class, and I could tell that Bella didn't like her. "May I pet your dog?" she asked in her commanding voice.

"Sure," I answered, afraid of the lecture to follow.

Debby bent down and reached for Bella's head. Bella ducked.

"Not good," said Debby. "She needs to get comfortable with strangers petting her. Work on that."

I nodded, knowing that mentioning Bella was head-shy was pointless. If Debby had sat down on the floor or had come toward Bella more slowly, she probably would have been fine. But the test required this, so I needed to find a way to help Bella overcome this phobia. I wondered if, before she was rescued, someone tried to grab her by the head. Did she survive because she learned very early that people were dangerous? She could have seen other dogs hung, run over, set on fire, stuffed into plastic bags, or shot. There was a reason it was called Dead Dog Beach.

As the weeks went by, Bella had to accept someone else brushing her and looking in her ears. She had to walk through a crowd of people and dogs and stay relaxed and at my side. She had to sit and stay while I dropped her leash and went to the other side of the room (she was great at this from agility), she had to come when called (again, pretty easy), she had to behave politely around other dogs as I greeted other handlers, and she could not react aggressively when a wheelchair came close to her or when someone made a loud noise by dropping a pan on the floor. Lastly, she couldn't go crazy when I left the room for three full minutes. She could get up, she could look toward the door, but she couldn't bark or show anxiety. I wasn't sure how this one would go.

I liked watching the other dogs and their handlers, except for the boxer. I couldn't understand why Debby allowed a dog who was this disturbed in our class. When we worked on the petting-another-dog exercise, she asked for volunteers to pet the boxer and offered a rubber arm and hand so that it was possible to do this without being bit. I was so not interested.

She called on one of the men in the class, who bravely took the rubber arm and stroked the dog's back. The dog lunged at the arm and bit into it. Like a flash, Debby was on top of him, pinning him down and yelling "No!" My heart was racing.

She asked me if I'd like to try. "Maybe he'll be less afraid with a woman."

"No thank you," I told her. "I'm not comfortable doing that."

"But you'll be safe. I'll hold onto him."

"No thank you," I repeated and she got it—I wouldn't do it. This may have been my first mistake.

Cathy and I talked about it on the way home. "Should I have tried?" I asked her.

"No way! I wouldn't do it. That dog is crazy."

The owner had told us that the dog had been fine until she and her husband went away for a week and left the dog with their twenty-year-old daughter. One night she had a wild party and after that the dog became aggressive and wouldn't allow anyone in the house except family. It was a sad story, but Debby reassured us that she had been working with this dog privately and would rehabilitate him.

"I don't see any progress, do you?" I asked Cathy.

"No, and if he gets near Brandon, it will all be over."

On the way home, we talked about Bella's head-shy issues. Debby had told me to desensitize her, but I wasn't sure how that was going to work. Bella was four years old, she had a safe and happy home, but still didn't want her head touched. That seemed to me to just be who she was.

Cathy reassured me that Bella's sweetness would win out. That she would be great with people even if they couldn't touch her head. I hoped she was right.

"How am I going to get Brandon to politely meet and greet male dogs?" she asked me. "You know how he is when we're out on walks."

I did. Brandon was like the chief. He had to be in the lead and was perfectly happy as long as Bella and Lela followed him. But when a male dog tried to walk past us on the street—even the other side of the street—he pulled on the leash and snarled. Not a CGC dog. More of an *I'd-like-to-rip-your-head-off* dog. Cathy hung on for dear life, she shouted at him, but like Bella, he was off in his own world and ignored her.

At home, Bob and I used treats to get Bella a tiny bit less uncomfortable about having her head touched. When she curled up next to us on the couch, she was fine, you could touch her anywhere. But if we stood and reached for her, she ducked. To expose her to more unfamiliar situations, I started bringing her into pet stores so that she'd have to pass other dogs in the aisles and would hopefully learn to trust me in new and strange environments. When she did a really good job, I let her pick out a bag of treats.

On our walks in the neighborhood, I used the *leave it* command when we passed other dogs and kept her on a short leash. That seemed to help, but I wasn't sure she'd be able to pass the test. It seemed to depend on the dogs she would have to interact with.

We finished the class in late spring, and Bob and I left Bella and Henry with our pet sitter while we took a vacation in Utah, hiking in Zion National Park and then volunteering at Best Friends Animal Sanctuary in Kanab, Utah. It was amazing. We walked dogs, cleaned pens, hauled water, played with puppies, helped out with the feral rabbits, and loved seeing the care the animals received. It was a beautiful and special place. We even attended a pet memorial service and a young woman stood up to talk about how much she loved her pet rat.

"He was so special," she said, tears running down her face. "I loved him so much."

I couldn't look at Bob because if I did, we'd both laugh, and we didn't want to be disrespectful. And I got it, I did, the loss of a pet rips you open.

When we got home, it was time to schedule the test. I called Debby and got a date in late June. In the few weeks leading up to the test, Bella and I practiced all the time.

Finally, we were in the waiting room of the facility, chatting with the receptionist who wanted to know all about Best Friends. Just as I was telling her about our volunteer work there, a woman and her dog came out of the training room and into the lobby, and the dog lunged at Bella. Bella's hair rose straight up and she growled, but did not counter-attack. Debby was behind the woman.

"Did you see that?" she yelled at me. "Bella is clearly unfit for testing."

"Excuse me?" I said, sure that I had misheard her.

"I can't test a dog who shows aggressive behavior."

"But the other dog came at her. She didn't bite him, just sent him a message to back off. She was protecting herself."

I looked up at the receptionist, hoping for an ally. She turned her head away and said nothing.

"You have some hard work to do," Debby informed me, "as this dog clearly has issues. And just so you know, they aren't things you'll be able to fix quickly. You've got months of work before you can even think about passing the CGC."

Somehow I got out of the building without either crying or shouting at her. As Bella sniffed around in the grass, I replayed what had just happened. She wasn't going to test Bella? She thought we wouldn't pass the test anytime soon? I couldn't believe it! I knew I didn't like her when I saw how she treated the boxer, but I didn't expect her to turn on us. I couldn't understand why she was so vindictive, why she took pleasure in putting us down.

As I forced myself to take deep, slow breaths, I admitted that Bella wasn't an easy dog, but I also knew, deep in my heart, that she was a good dog and that she would be a wonderful therapy dog. I had to find a way to pass the test. I had to get past Debby and whatever issues she had that had made her so sure we couldn't get certified.

I called Cathy when we got home. She couldn't believe it and reassured me that we would make it. But this was a huge glitch in our plans, as we wanted to get the dogs certified together. Brandon had passed the test while we were in Utah and was on his way to the next step of the certification process.

"She'll make it, Jean," Cathy told me, and I knew she was right. I also knew that I wouldn't be using Debby. I brooded about this for a few days, putting myself in a frenzy as I kept replaying what happened and thinking of really awful things that I wished I had said to Debby. But I finally came up with an idea: find another evaluator. Within ten minutes on the Internet, I had a list and called the two closest ones. Within an hour, Bella's test was scheduled for July, and the neat thing was that the test would be at the ASPCA facility where we had adopted our first dog, Angus. There was hope.

🐾 🐾

Bob, Bella, and I got to the ASPCA early and walked around the grounds. I was a wreck. Bob found a bench and read a book while Bella and I followed the evaluator, Pat, into the training room. She was soft spoken and kind. She liked Bella. Bella let her pet her on the head. I was holding my breath, trying to keep my expectations in line. She had us walk around the room. When I greeted her and shook her hand, Bella stood quietly by my side. I put her in a sit/ stay position and crossed the room. Bella stayed.

"Nice," said Pat. "She's well trained."

I nodded, afraid to open my mouth, afraid I would blow it by telling her how much this meant to me.

Then I had to leave Bella with her and go outside for three full minutes. I handed Pat the leash, told Bella she was a good girl, and walked out the door. I saw the look in her eyes, the questions: What are you doing? Why are you leaving me? Will you come back? I counted seconds, I hummed, I leaned toward the door wondering if Bella would bark or whine. If she did, it was over. If she pulled or acted upset, she would be disqualified. Finally, I heard Pat say, "Come back in."

I looked at Bella and she wagged her tail. Her eyes shimmered. "She missed you, but was fine."

I exhaled. For the last part of the test, another evaluator was supposed to bring his dog into the room to see how Bella would react. But Pat got a call on her cell phone that he couldn't make it, so she suggested we walk up the hill to the ASPCA kennels and walk past the outdoor runs. "That will give us a sense of her reaction," she said.

We passed Bob on his bench and Bella wanted to run to him. "This way," I told her, giving Bob a quick nod to let him know she was doing well.

As we approached the first run, I saw a beautiful collie run toward us. Bella hesitated, but didn't bark or snarl. It was like the ghost of Angus appearing to help us.

"Let her sniff him through the fence," said Pat, and I did. Bella was interested and, with the fence between them, she was not afraid. The collie wagged his tail and I silently thanked him. Further down the line, other dogs barked in their outdoor runs, and I wondered if Bella would have to meet them all.

"That's fine," Pat said. "She did a good job. You'll get the paperwork in the mail in a few weeks."

"She passed?"

"Yes. She did a great job. You've got a special dog here."

I wanted to throw my arms around her neck. I wanted to tell Pat what a relief this was. Instead, I simply said, "Thank you so much." I shook her hand. Bella waited politely by my side.

"Oh, what a good girl!" I told her as Pat went back to her car.

I gave her lots of praise and a handful of treats. "You did it," I whispered into her ear. "You did it."

When I straightened up, Bob didn't have to ask. He saw my face and Bella's tail wagging, and he knew.

Chapter 16

BONDING

There was something about showing up every week at an institution that changed things. After about three or four months, we were no longer visitors or outsiders and had become part of the fabric of the rehab facility. The administrators, nurses, and staff trusted us. The residents expected us, and knew exactly what to do when Shelby and Bella came into the room. And while the dogs were willing to visit with anyone, like us, they had their favorites.

Their favorite room was Alice and Jackie's. Jackie had bags of dog treats in her bedside table, and Alice's daughter, Nancy, a woman about our age, trumped that with organic peanut butter and molasses treats. When we got anywhere near their room, both dogs pulled. Bella was so excited, she jumped up on Jackie's bed while Jackie grinned from ear to ear and said, "Wait a minute. Wait a minute. I know what you want!"

Shelby wanted to jump up on the bed too, and a few times did, almost hurling Jackie off the other side. Deb and I laughed, while Nancy clapped her hands and her mother either slept through the whole thing or looked off into space.

Jackie was always elegantly dressed and upbeat, so at first I didn't understand why she was here. She reminded me of women in New York City—somehow intrinsically sophisticated—a pin matching her earrings, a silk scarf thrown casually around her neck. But then, in the middle of a visit, her words would become garbled and she'd say, "What's this thing here?" fingering Bella's harness, or, looking at Shelby, she'd start off on a thought but lose her way before it was over.

One day I asked her, "Are you all right?"

"No! No I'm not." And she hit herself in the head, adding, "It's not right in here. Not good. Not what I want."

I didn't know what to say so I stood there looking at her.

"Confused," she added.

"You feel confused?" asked Deb as the dogs waited to see if more treats would be offered.

Jackie nodded, and a sadness and tiredness overtook her face.

I put my hand on her shoulder and told her that we loved visiting her. She laid back on her bed, rested her head on her pillow, and looked out the window. We spent some time with Nancy, and I tried to talk with her mother, Alice, who didn't have any interest in the dogs but was very proud of her manicure.

"Your nails are beautiful," I told her, and she smiled. "I wish mine looked like that."

Alice said, "Of course you do," and we both laughed.

"We'll see you next week," said Deb, as we got our reluctant dogs to leave the room. It wasn't just the treats: Bella and Shelby both enjoyed having a fuss made over them and related to Jackie and Nancy because, like people, they knew when they were deeply admired. They recognized love.

Deb and I debriefed quickly in the hallway. "Can't beat that," she said.

"I know. But Jackie's having a tough time."

"It's hard to watch, isn't it?" asked Deb.

I nodded, thinking that she didn't need language to enjoy the dogs, but it must've been terrifying.

"I'd rather go quickly. Get hit by a truck."

"Would you stop it?" said Deb. "You've got to stick around so we can be roommates here."

"Now you're scaring me. I won't know who you are."

We continued down the hallway, Deb in the lead with her wonderful, warm invitation: "Would you like to see the dogs?" Even if the person couldn't talk, if we saw one glimmer of interest in their eyes, we were there.

We never woke people who were sleeping. We never disturbed the nurses or aides at their work. We didn't enter a room if the door was closed or the curtain pulled around the bed. And we quickly learned that a few of the residents disliked dogs. At the end of one hallway, near the nurses' station, there were almost always one or two residents in their wheelchairs. A nurse warned us that a new patient, Maxine, would probably yell at us if we got near her. She didn't just hate dogs, she hated everything, and was bent over in her wheelchair, muttering curses. She was so frail that I thought a strong wind would have pulverized her.

Deb took the warning as a dare. It was like someone saying, "Just try bringing your dog over here—there's no way you're going to get through to this person."

"Hi, Maxine," said Deb from a careful distance, Shelby at her side. Maxine snapped her head around and glared at Deb.

"I'm Deb and this is my dog, Shelby. We come here every week. Would you like to pet her?"

A string of garbled swear words erupted from her mouth, but Deb didn't back away.

"She's really soft."

Deb got Shelby a little closer and I noticed the nurses were watching too. Maxine had quite a reputation. She was weak but could still do some damage with her sharp nails.

Maxine's fingers twitched. "You could give her a treat," added Deb.

And miraculously her hand opened and Deb put a small treat on her palm. Shelby was on it in a flash, her wide soft tongue washing Maxine's hand.

"Oh!" she said, and then bent down closer to Shelby and said something I couldn't hear.

We waited and when she spoke again we heard her saying, "There you go, sweetheart."

The nurses' mouths were open, and Deb slowly stood and told Maxine that we looked forward to seeing her next week. Maxine slumped back down in her wheelchair, the space around her once again closed in. Bella and I watched, but didn't go near her.

As we went around the corner into another wing, I told Deb, "That was amazing!"

"I know," she said, smiling. "My girl can do just about anything." And she could.

This made me think of love as a multiplier. Deb loved Shelby so much, and they were deeply connected in so many ways, that love could break through even the bitterness that surrounded Maxine. It was a force to be reckoned with.

I was still too new in this work to see the ways it was changing me, and given my almost twenty years as a career coach, and having written two books in the field, I still expected in that first summer after having lost my job, that I would be able to replace it with something similar. I researched local outplacement firms, sent out résumés, networked to seek out the decision makers, attended job search groups, offered to speak on career topics, and ultimately drove myself a bit nuts. I couldn't let go of the feeling that only this kind of work would give me a sense of purpose and belonging. I couldn't admit, but still believed, that I was owed a job as a career coach.

Two things shocked me out of this belief: First, I finally got an offer from one of my former company's competitors. They offered me three days of work a week—half of it in Rhode Island and the other half in Connecticut. Both locations were about an hour drive from my home. When I got the offer, the woman who would have been my boss said, "I'm really embarrassed about the money," and then quoted me a daily fee that was what I had earned in the 1970s. I asked her if she could come up a bit, and she promised to get back to me in a few days. As I thought about it—doing the long drive, having a client load again, adjusting to all the rules and regulations that go with the outplacement industry—I realized money wasn't the problem. The job was. I didn't want to go back. I couldn't go back.

I called her the next day, thanked her for the offer, and declined. She understood and told me to stay in touch if I changed my mind. It's always hard to say no, to walk away, but I knew I had done the right thing. The second thing that took a bit longer but still helped me say goodbye to this phase of my life, was getting rehired by my former company. The work was awful, as I went with other career counselors to companies that were letting staff go, and after each employee was notified, he or she had the option to meet with one of us to go over their outplacement program. We were there to help them see that all was not lost. It rarely worked, as most people were too angry, too hurt, or too shocked to hear a word we said. Therapists were there, too, to pick up the pieces.

This tenuous connection to my former company helped me remember that I was not alone in struggling to get over job loss, and that in many ways I had outgrown this work in the outplacement industry. But I held on to this job this first summer in our new home because it gave me a link to my past life.

Chapter 17

THE THERAPY DOG CERTIFICATION TEST

Fall 2011
Yardley, Pennsylvania

We were lucky that in Pennsylvania where we lived there was a wonderful therapy dog organization called Bright and Beautiful Therapy Dogs, Inc. They made the process simple and had been certifying therapy dogs since 1992. On their website, Cathy and I found a self-test that included the basics of what would be expected on the real test. As I read down the list, only one item concerned me: "What happens when your dog sees another dog?" And the multiple choice answers:

A. He exhibits mild curiosity and wags his tail.

B. He growls, snarls, and drags you down the street.

Oh, boy, did we have a challenge. Bella was for sure a "B" dog, unless she met a dog she knew and liked; then she squealed, flipped onto her back, and writhed in total ecstasy like an electric eel. The bad news was that she was basically fearful, and this turned into aggression toward dogs she didn't know. She was especially afraid of large dogs, and dogs of any size who were assertive and in her face. But the good news was I knew she genuinely liked people, and with Bob and me now the grandparents of three young children, I also knew she was good with kids. And of course, she'd had a lot of training from our two years in agility, so she paid attention to me and wanted to please. I hoped that the strong relationship between us would pull us through. I prayed the good outweighed the bad.

Like preparing for the CGC, we practiced endlessly. We took walks in new neighborhoods, we went to PetSmart, we drilled every night after dinner, we sought out kids on bikes and skateboards, we walked in town where there was traffic and more people, we brought Bella with us on our monthly car trips to our house in Connecticut where we hoped to move once we retired, or I should say once Bob retired. I hated the word, hated the concept, as I liked to work. And at almost sixty-five, I still felt energetic and committed to my work as a career coach and author.

But when I sat still, when I thought about this carefully, I admitted to myself that I was frustrated, that my world was too small, and that much of the joy had gone out of my work. I was going through the motions, I looked forward to cancellations (my case load had doubled), and I was always behind. This made me bored and cranky. I was still good with my clients, as I had a deep empathy for people who had lost their jobs. From more than seventeen years of experience, I knew how to motivate them and help them with creative solutions. I listened carefully, but I felt worn down and trapped. I didn't see choices, or a way to make this job better, and I felt entitled to this job. The worse it got, the stronger I felt about this.

I knew I was in trouble. One of the most annoying phrases I delighted in telling my clients was, "All jobs are temporary." But, like Alice in Wonderland, I didn't heed my own advice. I didn't prepare myself for the very real possibility that I would lose my job. As the fall progressed, I had received emails and attended meetings about a firm my company planned to acquire. It was a smart way to reduce the competition, and this other firm was skilled at doing more with less, skilled at streamlining procedures to increase profits. It all came down to math, not what real services were offered to people in transition. But I figured if I could adjust to the new system, I would be retained and personnel from the company we were buying would have to go. That made sense.

And I was proud of what I'd done in my work. On top of the daily counseling load, I had designed classes that were practical and popular, facilitated a weekly team, and had written a book on getting through job loss that had received strong media attention and was given out to all the career consultants at last year's annual meeting. I thought of these things like insurance that would prevent my name from ending up on the list of those being let go.

Each day, however, was a bit like walking on quicksand. It made me tense. I told the office administrator that I was going to lose my job. She laughed and told me I was crazy. Sometimes I told her that I was going to be notified that week or that day. She rolled her eyes and told me to get a life. I put a photo of Bella on my desk. I told my clients about preparing for the therapy dog test. I told them we were going to volunteer at the local hospital. Some thought this was wonderful, while others looked at me as if I were losing it. It was the one thing in my life, other than our wonderfully expanding family, that pulled me out of this trap, that made me happy.

Cathy and I walked our dogs together, both of us worried about their interactions with other dogs. I thought she had an advantage, as Brandon was a bit older and his personality was more laid back than Bella's. Kim and I often called him Mr. Cool

119

because he had a confident, relaxed manner. But not my Bella. With those wonderful terrier genes, she was wired. She was pure energy, and I was so glad that I'd started letting her off-leash where it was safe: in the woods, or in the large field near our house. I often brought a ball thrower and hurled a tennis ball as far as I could, and off she went—a streak of white—running back to me with her prize. She never tired of this game. In fact, nothing seemed to really tire her out except a full day at doggie daycare. Then she could barely stand.

On a warm day in late fall, Cathy and I, plus our two dogs, headed up to Doylestown to take the therapy dog certification test. It was being held in a fire station, and we knew that there would be at least two evaluators and a few other dogs. She and I talked nonstop during the forty-five minute drive, burning off a bit of our nervousness, afraid of the disappointment if we failed.

🐾 🐾

Cathy parked her car and we got out, giving the dogs plenty of time to sniff around and do their business. Cathy's appointment was right before mine, and I was happy to see a bench outside the firehouse where Bella and I could hang out in the October sun.

"You are going to be great," I told Cathy, and then they were called in, and Bella and I waited. It seemed like forever. I talked to Bella, I sat, I got up, we practiced a few commands, and then I told myself that I needed to relax. Such good advice, but impossible to follow. Finally, Cathy and Brandon came out. Cathy was grinning ear to ear and Brandon was his usual nothing-can-bother-me self.

"You passed!" I said, and she nodded.

I gave her a quick hug and one of the evaluators came to the door: "Jean and Bella."

"Here we are," I said, and we followed her inside the building.

I had to fill out a form and Bella stayed quietly beside me despite the two other dogs in the room. They were far enough away that Bella ignored them.

"Let's have you walk around the room with Bella on a loose leash," said one of the evaluators.

I did this and then she had me put her in a sit-stay and I had to drop the leash and walk to other side of the room. She then had to come to me when I called her. She was perfect!

I was asked to have her sit on my left while one of the evaluator dogs, a huge German Shepherd, walked in a circle around us. I saw Bella's hair rise and I repeated *sit* and *stay*, but when the dog got behind us, it was too much for her and she got up and whirled around.

"Bella, sit!" And she did. She didn't growl, didn't go after the other dog, but was clearly afraid.

The other evaluator put a chunk of salami on the floor and asked me to walk Bella past it and tell her to leave it. I could see her interest in the meat, but I kept her moving and she obeyed. Then both evaluators came at Bella with a walker and a wheelchair and dropped metal pans on the floor. She was calm and collected and looked up at me to see if this was all right.

"Good girl," I told her.

I also had to walk up to one of the evaluators who had her dog with her, shake her hand, and Bella had to stay calmly at my side. She did this. I tried desperately to read the faces and body language of those two women, but couldn't. Would they say no because Bella didn't stay seated when the dog circled her? Why couldn't they have used a smaller dog, one that Bella wasn't afraid of?

I don't remember the rest of the test; it flew by in a blur. Finally, they called us over to the desk and handed me some paperwork.

"Did she pass?" I asked, with my heart in my mouth.

They smiled at me and one said, "Yes. She is going to be a fine therapy dog, but since she's not perfect with other dogs, it's your job to take her to places where this won't be an issue. Don't volunteer at the courthouse where dogs are in close quarters. And keep working on her social interaction with others dogs. She is clearly a sweet dog and great with people."

I was wondering if it was okay to hug them. I was wondering if my feet were still on the floor. How could it be that they saw in Bella what I had known all along, even at our worst moments? At almost five years old, she had a new calling. A job. With my temporary certificate in hand, I walked out into the autumn sunshine where Cathy and Brandon were waiting. Without words, she knew the answer and we gave each other a big hug. We did it! We both had certified therapy dogs.

Chapter 18

WHEN A DOG IS
LIKE A TEENAGER

Fall 2012
Stonington, Connecticut

Anyone who's had dogs, and especially people who have trained their dogs, knew these moments: the well-behaved dog who never stole food, but then eats all the hors d'oeuvres on the coffee table when you scooted into the kitchen to get someone a refill of their drink. Or the dog who jumped up on a friend when they came to your house, or ran out in the street, totally ignoring you. In Bella's case, when excited, she nipped at the bottoms of people's pants. She didn't hurt anyone, but some people don't like their pants nibbled. Over and over, we pretended to be strangers coming to the door. We rang the bell, and then whoever was in the house with Bella said, "Stay!" The moment the door opened, she hurled herself at the intruder/guest and squealed. Even if it was just us.

My training mantra was *consistency and repetition*. Do the same things and continue to do them over and over. That was the key. Certain commands like *sit* were rock solid, but the ones I forgot to practice were like algebraic equations—quickly forgotten. I moved to plan b and put Bella in a bedroom when the grandkids arrived, as her greetings made a whirling dervish look sluggish.

Now it was the fall of 2012, almost Bella's one-year anniversary of being certified, and we'd survived Hurricane Sandy. Because we were close to the water, we had to evacuate and spent two nights at Bob's sister's place on higher ground. But we had been lucky—our house was unharmed. Water from the cove flooded the field opposite our house, but not us. It was a terrible day, a Nor'easter was hitting us hard, and it was windy, cold, and wet. Our power was out. We were glad to be back home but there wasn't much we could do. I made tea and toasted bagels on the gas grill outside, and we had soup for dinner. It was like camping and was fun for about one meal, but after a few days, it was tiring and we were worried about the dropping temperatures.

I needed to get out of the house, so I told Bella we were going to work. She looked at me but didn't move, didn't do her usual okay-let's-get-going dance.

"Come on," I urged, shuffling her out the door and into the car. I checked to make sure I had my blue volunteer jacket, treats, poop bags, a towel for Bella, and my cell phone. I was good to go. The hospital parking lot was full near the volunteer office, so I drove into the parking garage and finally found a place on the second floor.

As I reached across the back seat to slide her Easy-Walk harness over her head, she backed into the far corner.

"Right here!" I commanded in a don't-mess-with-me voice.

She moved further away.

"Hey! Get over here."

When that didn't work, I grabbed her collar and pulled her to my side of the car. Now I was irritated.

"You need to listen to me!" I told her as she avoided eye contact with me. I could hear my mother's voice in mine, as well as echoes of the times I had reprimanded my children. Part of me realized this was pointless, while another part didn't care. Bella was supposed to obey. I attached her leash and gave it a tug. She jumped out of the car, sulking like a teenager.

We took the elevator down to the ground floor, ran through the rain to the volunteer office, and signed in. By the time we were up on the fifth floor, we had both recovered. We visited an elderly woman whose daughter was sitting next to her. As soon as she saw Bella, the daughter said, "Oh, I miss my dogs!"

I asked about her dogs and found out she lived in Vermont. I gently steered Bella toward her mother, who didn't seem one bit interested in a dog, but who did want to talk. I listened, answered the daughter's questions about Bella, and after a "Nice to meet you," moved on.

We saw a few more people and then entered a dimly lit room. In the far bed was a woman of about forty, her head turned to the side, her whole bed lined with blue rubber mats. A padded cell.

"Would you like a visit from a dog?" I asked softly.

Her eyes moved to my face and that was it.

"This is Bella, if you'd like to see her."

Nothing.

I stood at the foot of the bed and waited. I wondered if she was in terrible pain.

"Nice to meet you," I whispered, and we left.

The hallways were busy. Patients were being transported on gurneys and the cleaning crew was taking out mountains of garbage bags. After visiting several more patients, we got into the elevator and Bella relaxed. I could feel her unwinding. I didn't know what this work did to her but it was demanding: so many sights, and smells, and noises, and unpredictability. With her keen sense of smell, it must have been like me going to a rock concert without ear plugs—totally overwhelming.

"One more stop, girlfriend," I told her, glancing at my watch. I tried to keep our visits to an hour so she didn't burn out.

As we entered the Cancer Center and passed the private rooms, I realized I was looking for Gloria, a young woman we had met a few weeks ago. She had been lying on a bed, wrapped in a white blanket, with tears streaming down her face. I had hesitated at the door, not wanting to embarrass her or intrude, but she had turned her head and when she saw Bella, she simply said, "Oh."

"This is Bella," I had said, moving a bit closer. "Would you like to see her?"

"Oh, yes," she had responded, and Bella gently put her paws up on the edge of her bed and let her pet her head. I was speechless.

"She is so cute!"

I then told Gloria that Bella had been rescued from Puerto Rico, and she told me that was where she was from. As we talked, her hand never left Bella. She was connected to her soft fur and strong, lean body. She stopped crying.

"I wish my daughter could see her."

"How old is she?"

"Ten."

And then we had the brilliant idea of taking a picture of Bella and her on her cell phone. She handed me her phone and I took the picture. When she looked at the photo, she smiled and said, "She is going to love this."

I had nodded, beaming like a proud parent, thinking to myself, *Look what you've done, Bella. Look how Gloria went from tears to smiling. Look how you changed everything.*

We didn't talk about her cancer or her treatment. Just the dog, a wonderful dog who got over her shyness and had let Gloria share her sadness with her. When it was time to leave, Gloria said "Thank you." And that was all I had needed. The rain, having no power at home, Bella's stubbornness, and anything else that was bothering me was gone.

This time, all the private rooms were empty and only four people sat in the infusion room, plus the nurses. Bella put her paws on the side of these patients' recliners and I handed them treats to feed to her. While we were at one end of the room, another patient arrived—a large, strong man with huge hands and long hair pulled back into a pony tail. I didn't see him at first, but he saw us and said, "Hey, little white dog!"

I remembered him from several weeks back, a dog person who raised German Shepherds.

We went over to his chair once he was hooked up and chatted about dog temperaments. He said, "My dogs never bit anyone who didn't deserve it."

"What?" I asked, startled.

"Yeah. The guy who tried to break into my house. He got a nice deep puncture wound in the butt."

I laughed, and as the woman in the chair next to his joined in, it felt like a party. We were trading stories, being pulled into each other's lives.

I told them about my sister's dog, who bit the liquor man and a visiting minister when we were kids.

"They know," said the huge man.

"But not the Fuller Brush Man," I added.

"Oh, that takes me back," said the woman, and we discussed the neat traveling cases those salesmen had—full of brushes of all kinds. It seemed like a magical and distant world.

So, while powerful chemicals dripped into their veins, as a war to survive was being fought, we transported ourselves back to the 1950s. And Bella was the catalyst. She was the one who had started this.

"As a kid I was up before 5 a.m.," said the huge man, "and hitched a ride on the milk truck. It was our way to get places."

I could see him running after the truck, could see that boy now in this man, just as I could hear the glass bottles clanking in their wire baskets. And I was struck how, at that moment, his youth was there. It shined through his face, changing him. Bella stared at my pocket, wondering when the next treat would appear.

"I didn't forget you," I said, giving her one last treat as we said good-bye.

Bella curled up in the back seat of the car and took a nap. She had done her thing and now it was time to rest.

"Good girl," I told her. "You did a fine job."

She closed her eyes and rested her head on her hind feet.

As I was driving home, I thought about what a man had said to us as we left the Cancer Center waiting room: "You come here to make people feel better? Is that right?"

Without asking, he had taken the leash from my hands and held that link to Bella.

"Yes," I had said, "that's Bella's job."

What I didn't say was that it was reciprocal. That coming here and to the rehab facility made me feel better, too. It never failed. My teenager had a gift.

Bob holding Bella on our deck on her first day at our home, May 2007.

Bella sitting on our deck as a puppy, getting to know her new backyard.

Angus, the dog we had before Bella, walks down our street in a blizzard.

Bella and our cat, Henry, get acquainted.

Bella on high alert, ready to play. Image courtesy of Leasajo Hall.

Bella and I join Deb and Shelby at the Starfish House where we volunteer every week. Image courtesy of Leasajo Hall.

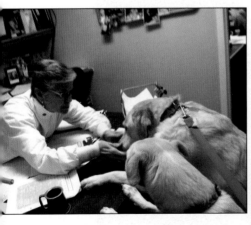

Bella and Shelby get treats from Jan, the nurse coordinator at Starfish.

Bella and Shelby have a weekly visit with Abby at Starfish.

Bella suns herself after a swim.

Bella and Henry put their heads together.

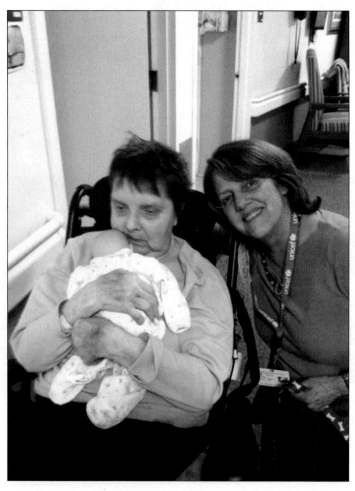

Beverly and I comfort the "baby" at Starfish. Beverly becomes my favorite.

Bella touches a resident's hand at Starfish. Image courtesy of Leasajo Hall.

Bella in front of our rhododendrons. Image courtesy of Leasajo Hall.

Bella and I take a rest while out hiking.

Bella running full out at Barn Island, Connecticut.

Bella, after running loose and swimming at Barn Island, Connecticut.

Liam meets Bella at Deans Mill School. Image courtesy of Grace White, *The Westerly Sun*.

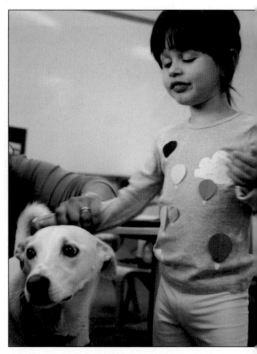

Annelise, a legally blind seven-year-old girl, gets her first touch of Bella's back. Image courtesy of Grace White, *The Westerly Sun*.

Bella enjoys playing hide-and-seek at Deans Mill School. Image courtesy of Grace White, *The Westerly Sun*.

Bella reads a book with Austin, Deans Mill School. Image courtesy of Leasajo Hall.

Bella really likes the story Liam is reading to her at Deans Mill School. Image courtesy of Leasajo Hall.

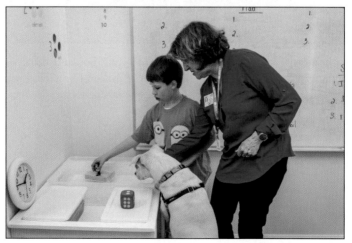

Bella puts her paws up to see Liam's experiment at Deans Mill School. Image courtesy of Leasajo Hall.

Bella has a good time with Annelise, who is sitting on Mrs. Scott's lap. Image courtesy of Mrs. Scott.

Bella and Henry have a nap together.

Bella cocks her head as if asking, "Are you listening?" Image courtesy of Leasajo Hall.

Kat and I, plus Boo and Bella, walk down a hallway at the local hospital. Image courtesy of Bill Hanrahan.

Chapter 19

REVOLVING DOOR

Fall–Winter 2011
Yardley, Pennsylvania

I was proud of my work, in particular how I related to corporate executives, hourly workers, scientists with PhDs, Wall Street traders, welders, you name it. What made me good at this were two things: I was an extrovert and loved meeting new people, and I listened carefully. I took notes. I listened for what my clients said and didn't say, and I watched their faces, their body language. Sometimes I thought of myself as yeast; I had a quick wit, a good sense of humor, and I used that in work where many people were hurt or discouraged. This helped them get over the shock of job loss, and encouraged them to start recovering and look for new work.

Some days I forgot about the shadow hanging over the company I worked for. I forgot about the merger, the rumors, the threats of job loss, and just did my work. On this particular Thursday afternoon in late October, I was meeting with a woman who had to be at least seventy years old. She was in a panic and had taken a job at a local warehouse, moving boxes of books. I couldn't see her moving much of anything, but she was so desperate, so sure she was facing immediate ruin, that she leapt at this low-paying job where she couldn't succeed.

"How can you do that job?" I asked her.

"It hurts," she told me, "but I do my best."

"But you've done payroll and accounts receivable and payable. Wouldn't that pay more and not be so physically demanding?"

She nodded but I could see she didn't believe she'd ever find a job like her last one. In her mind, it was over.

I waited to see if she'd say anything more. She didn't.

"May I ask you something?" I said.

"Sure."

"Do you think some companies hire people with a lot of experience?"

"Of course."

"And you have a lot of experience, right?"

She nodded.

"So, while you're working at the warehouse, could we make a plan to get you back to a higher paying, more appropriate job?"

"I guess so."

I waited again.

"You've got to want this and believe it can happen or it won't," I told her.

Tears streamed down her face. She took a Kleenex from the box on my table.

"I know," she whispered. "But why did they let me go?"

"You'll never really know, but I can tell you this. I work with hundreds of people every year who have been let go. And you know what? They're really good at their jobs. They're smart, motivated, loyal, and they still lose their jobs. That's just the way it is. At some point, you have to let go of that question and move on."

I saw a faint light in her eyes, as though she believed me. Before the light went out, I added, "Let's set one simple task for the next week, okay? I sent you notes on your résumé, so your job is to go through them, see what makes sense, and email me a new draft. Can you do that?"

She nodded.

I got out my calendar and we scheduled a time to meet the following week. When she stood, I gave her a hug.

"Thank you," she said. "I feel a bit better."

I opened my office door, telling her that I would see her next week, and there in a cubical right outside the door was my boss. She was looking at me.

"Oh," I said, surprised to see her there, as she worked in another office.

"Got a minute?" she asked.

"I'm just going to the kitchen to rinse my mug out. Come with me."

"Let's go into your office," she said.

Warning bells were clanging in my head.

"No."

She looked stunned but not entirely surprised.

"We need to talk."

I had turned to stone and couldn't move.

"Would you go to Roger's office?" she asked, as though she were speaking to a wild animal or a child on the verge of a tantrum.

I nodded. I liked Roger. He ran the office but wasn't my boss.

She knocked on his door and, as we walked in, he turned his head and wouldn't look at me.

"Jean and I are going to have our meeting here," she told him. She sat and pointed to a chair. I didn't want to sit. Roger pulled his chair over and I was trapped. I sat.

"As you know, Jean, we're acquiring another firm and that means we have to make changes."

I glanced over at Roger and saw tears in his eyes. I looked back to my boss who showed no emotion. No concern. She had a job to do and would do it. The end. I saw that she had a packet of papers for me and I knew how this story went.

"You can work until the end of the year but then your job is done."

"My job or me?" I asked, glaring at her.

"Well, you know what I mean. You in your job."

Roger was now crying.

I got up and hit him softly on the arm.

"Roger, you can't cry. I'm doing my best to hold it together, but stop it. Stop right now."

My boss made a fatal mistake. She said, "Look at you. You've lost your job and you're concerned about Roger."

I turned to her, wanting to strike her, wanting to smack that smug I'm-in-charge-and-you've-just-lost-your-job expression off her uncaring face.

"That's the kind of office this is," I said in a low voice, my most threatening voice. "We care about each other."

Roger wiped his eyes and said, "I thought Jean told you a few years ago that if she were to lose her job, she didn't want to be notified in a meeting. I thought she asked you to call her on the days she works at home."

"Well, I know but—"

I didn't listen to the rest. I announced, "I have to go. I have an appointment." Which I did, with my chiropractor.

"But we haven't gone over your package."

"Don't want to. I'll read it and will email my questions to you."

I took the packet, headed for the door, and turned back.

"Thank you, Roger. Your support means a lot."

I got back into my office, grabbed my purse and jacket, and walked out the door. By the time I got to my car, I was shaking.

Furious. I sat still for a moment and called Bob on my cell phone. I told him I lost my job.

"Oh, I'm so sorry," he said. "Come home."

"Got the chiropractor."

"Okay, but after that. It's going to be all right."

I started my car and pulled out of the office park. Now, not my office park, not my building, not my anything.

It was a quick drive to the chiropractor's. "Really?" I said out loud all the way there. "Really? Me, really?"

When I was face down on the adjustment table, I told my chiropractor. She was a wonderful woman and told me she was glad I was there.

"I feel as though I'm on the edge of a cliff, falling," I told her.

"You are," she answered, "but for right now I want you to imagine that you're falling into a deep pool of water. Lovely, warm, blue-green water. And you're safe."

I felt her skilled hands on my back. I imagined the water. And my tears soaked through the paper under my face.

Sometimes it's good when things aren't too easy. Passing the Canine Good Citizen and Therapy Dogs tests wasn't easy, but I was not prepared for how difficult it would be to start volunteering at the hospital with Bella. And without realizing it, I wanted something to be easy, as I was hurting from having been notified a few weeks earlier that my job of sixteen years would be over at the end of the year. I was no longer needed. No reason, no apologies, just good-bye. I got into a useless fight with my boss over the severance package and finally came to the conclusion that I had to let it go. I had to move on.

And on some unconscious level, I think I knew all this was coming because, in my first book, *Eliminated! Now What?*, published a year earlier, I'd started the first chapter:

> *There are almost always signs before you lose your job, but many times you don't see them until after the fact. So you're called into a meeting with your boss, and someone from HR is sitting there as well, and they both look as if they'd like to sink through the floor. You are politely told to have a seat. And as you wonder why you're there, you're told that, due to: restructuring, downsizing, acquisition, loss of business or the current financial crisis, you're no longer needed. And then they might reassure you that this has nothing to do with your performance, in fact . . . (this is the point where you can't hear anymore and you're sure this is a bad dream or hallucination). So their mouths keep moving but nothing is sinking in. . . . in the course of less than an hour your whole world has been turned upside down.*

It's now December 2011, and in the middle of preparations for Christmas, getting ready to put our house on the market, and working the last few weeks of my job, my friend and neighbor, Cathy, and I have been running back and forth to St. Mary Medical Center. We got our TB tests done (not once, but twice), we had mountains of paperwork to hand in—including our dog's veterinary records so that the hospital could verify they were up to date on all their shots—we and our dogs had to have photos taken for our ID badges, and we were required to attend a half-day volunteer orientation.

At this orientation, which we attended without the dogs, we learned about patient confidentiality, hospital codes—including a dress code: no jeans or open-toed shoes—and which areas we could visit as well as the ones we couldn't, like maternity and the surgical floor. We heard about a wonderful program they'd recently initiated called No One Dies Alone. I was amazed there were volunteers who sat with people who were dying, people who had no family with them. The hospital was like a complicated machine. There were so many needs filled by volunteers, from delivering magazines and books to escorting patients in wheelchairs. Then we were told that when we heard the Brahms lullaby over the PA system, a baby had just been born.

As the days shortened and the nights grew cold, I realized this was my life raft, my future. The one bright spot on the horizon. Even then I found it amazing that my dog, my bundle of crazy energy, was saving me.

PART IV: WORKING GIRL

Chapter 20

EXPECT NOTHING, BE SURPRISED

Fall 2012
Stonington, Connecticut

Hospitals are made of different communities, and physical therapy was one of the hopeful places, communal and often full of activity. Bella liked going up what I called "the stairs to nowhere." And she was fond of platforms from her agility days. I was a great believer in the "nothing is wasted" philosophy, so Bella's agility training kept her focused on me, and she read the slightest changes in my body or facial expressions. She often knew before I did what my next move was.

But physical therapy was also a place where fear and pain battled it out with healing and recovery. It reminded me of what my mother told me about grief: you have to get through it. There were no detours or shortcuts.

A woman who had had a stroke sat slumped in her wheelchair. The physical therapist tried to get her to use her right hand, which lay abandoned in her lap. Bella and I approached from the right.

"Would you like to see the dog?" I asked.

She nodded and a flicker of light shone in her eyes. At least this was something different.

Bella wasn't too sure about the wheelchair, but I lured her next to this patient's right leg with a treat. She was watching Bella intently.

"Try to pet the dog," instructed the therapist, and the woman froze, as if this was too much to process.

I asked her, "May I put a treat in your hand for Bella?"

A nod.

And as Bella nudged her hand with her nose, as she gently got the treat, it looked to me like a finger or two moved.

"Again?" I asked, and we did it again. And once more.

Like a child who sat obediently in school all morning, Bella needed to burn off steam. After saying good-bye to the patient, I let her fly up and down the stairs to nowhere before moving on.

When I asked the next patient, an elderly man, if he'd like to see the dog, he didn't respond. I gave him a few minutes to see if he would change his mind, but he looked blankly ahead. I reminded myself that he may be in pain. Or he may be overcome by fear at what his life had become. I didn't know, and I realized it was not my job to figure it out. I was simply here with Bella, encouraging her to do her thing. Having worked as a career counselor for many years, I reminded myself that all jobs had aspects that were ordinary and uninspiring. There was no reason why pet therapy should be any different.

We left the physical therapy ward to see if there were other patients who would like to have Bella stop by. If I saw a doctor in a room, I didn't go in. I knew they had too much to do and wouldn't welcome a distraction. If the nurses were really busy, we

140

stayed out of their way. But many times, seeing into a patient's room was difficult, so I learned to walk a little way in and then ask my question: "Want a visit from a therapy dog?"

In this particular room, a woman in her early forties with her arm in a sling and an IV pole next to her bed said, "Oh, yes! Bring him in."

"This is Bella," I said, letting her figure out the gender issue.

A nurse came in to check the IV drip and I asked her if it was okay if Bella put her paws up on the bed. She nodded, but I hesitated, as this patient's legs were so white they looked like bandages. The woman decided to sit up and swung her legs over the side of the bed. I gave her a treat to give Bella, and as soon as Bella ate it, her hand moved in one swift motion to Bella's head. She ducked.

"You can cure that, you know," she told me.

Not really, is what I thought, but I said, "I'm working on it."

"You have to desensitize her."

I used my standard defense about Bella being a rescue, while realizing this was a somewhat hollow excuse. Bella was either born or dumped on Dead Dog Beach in Puerto Rico, but I didn't know how long she had been there. Now she was five years old. Would early trauma still affect her?

I wanted to tell this woman that she had let Leonard pet her on the head. I wanted to tell her that Bella had come a long way from a puppy we had to keep on a leash or in a crate in the house to a dog who walked by my side with no leash. I wanted to say: maybe you smell funny or perhaps there is something about you she just doesn't like. But I didn't. Instead, I gave her a few more moments, told her it was nice to meet her, and left.

Bella and I had a super game of tug of war in the hallway, and I told her that she did a really good job. It would be so much easier if she didn't mind being touched on the head, but that wasn't who she was. The way I figured it, some of this work had to be on her terms.

🐾 🐾

When I visited the hospital with Kat and one of her Australian Shepherds, Wren or Boo, I noticed two things: one was that Kat's take on this work was that everyone needed to see a dog, so if there were families in the hallway, or one of the janitors taking out trash, they got the same attention as the patients. They were just as important and perhaps needed a dog visit more than some of the patients. The other thing I noticed was that she was shy; it was hard for her to go into a room, but with a dog, she could do it.

I was not shy, but there was so much to learn both about this work and about how hospitals were run, that I sometimes hesitated before walking into a room if one glance gave me the feeling the person inside might be disturbed by a dog visit. Over time, I got better at this, but at almost the one-year mark as a therapy dog team, Bella and I were still on the steep part of the learning curve.

Kat's dogs were well trained and beautiful. Their coats were luxurious and they knew some cute tricks. Kat said, "Boo, time for bed!" and she dropped to the floor and closed her eyes. Wren knew how to open closed cabinet doors. Bella's repertoire was mostly: sit, stay, paws up, lie down, shake, and up. I could also put a treat on her paw when she was lying down and tell her to leave it, and she did. As I told the kids in the bite-prevention programs, "She's not a circus dog. Tricks aren't really important, but coming to visit people is."

As I drove Bella to the hospital on a warm fall day, I realized that it had been one year since I was notified my job was about to be over. Weeks had gone by and I hadn't thought about this, hadn't replayed the conversation with my boss, hadn't had fantasies of revenge. I knew time helped create perspective, but I believed it was this work with Bella that was healing me, not time alone. Having something that I loved to do, having a purpose, getting out of the house and meeting other people, had put my layoff in perspective. I could almost see it as business as usual.

Plus, I now had another job. I had designed a course for "mature" job seekers, a class I'd named Boomers Back to Work! And starting in November, in just a few weeks, I would be teaching the first class. I'd already had meetings at the four CTWorks! (unemployment) offices to share with the staff what my course was about, and almost every day, I reviewed my PowerPoint presentation and the handouts. I was ready to jump back into a field I loved, but this time as an independent contractor. It felt really good and eclipsed the occasional work I was doing for my former company.

Bella and I signed in at the hospital volunteer office and had a nice chat with Jamie, the head of the office. She loved Bella and didn't get upset that Bella did things on her own terms. I handed her a pile of magazines I'd brought from home so they could distribute them to the patients.

"Any requests?" I asked.

She shook her head. "Not today."

So Bella and I took the elevator to the fifth floor, visited a few people, and were just about to head down to the Cancer Center when a woman in the far bed of a room we were passing asked us to come in.

"Sure," I said, and as we entered the room, the woman in the near bed sat up and yelled: "What is a dog doing here?"

I caught my breath and did my best to answer quietly. "She's a therapy dog. We're here every week."

"Get that filth out of here!"

The woman in the far bed watched this drama unfold. It was a lot more exciting than daytime TV.

"We won't come near you," I told her, "but I'm going to visit this other patient, and we'll only be a few minutes."

"I'm calling the nurse. Dogs don't belong in hospitals."

I ignored her and introduced Bella to the other patient. She apologized for her roommate.

"Don't worry about it," I told her, "it's very rare."

And it was. This was the first time it had ever happened.

"She has such a sweet face," said the patient in the far bed.

"She is sweet," I told her, and as we were leaving she said, "I appreciate your service. It's so kind of you."

Holding on to that affirmation, I quickly left the room, wondering if I was going to run into a nurse or be kicked off the floor. Out in the hallway, I told Bella she was a good girl and filled her water bowl, a collapsible cloth one, from the drinking fountain and let her have a good drink.

"One more stop, girlfriend," I told her, as we still had to visit the Cancer Center. One of the patients we had seen for weeks was standing by the Cancer Center reception desk. She had on a new wig and looked terrific.

"Look at you!" I said, as she bent to pat Bella.

"I'm done with chemo," she said, beaming.

"Congratulations. I'm so glad to hear it."

I realized I had never seen her standing before, only seated in a recliner, attached to an IV.

"I'll miss Bella," she said, "but I'm glad to be out of here."

We chatted for a few more minutes, and as I turned to take Bella into the infusion room, she had one more thing to say: "Keep up the visits. You have no idea what they mean when you're fighting cancer."

I gave her a hug and Bella got an extra treat just for being who she was.

Chapter 21

WE GO TO SCHOOL

Winter 2013
Stonington, Connecticut

We had done several bite-prevention programs at preschools and kindergartens, but we'd never been part of an ongoing program at a school. A regular. I got the word out to my dog network that I was looking for an elementary school where Bella and I could volunteer. I loved the hospital and rehab facility, but I sensed Bella's gifts were particularly suited to children, and it would make a good contrast with people who were sick, old, or dying.

Despite numerous follow-up calls, I couldn't get into a school in my local community, but did connect with a woman, Carol, in another part of Connecticut who had founded the pet therapy program in an elementary school about seven years ago. She was a pro. After we'd spoken on the phone a few times, she asked me to send her Bella's paperwork, which I did. Then we scheduled a visit for right after the holidays so I could shadow her as she made her rounds with her dog, Max. Bella was not invited to this first meeting.

On a cold January morning, I went into the school, signed in at the front desk, and received my visitor's badge. Carol came down the hall with Max, and I was struck by how comfortable he looked, as if he were taking a stroll outside. He greeted me with a typical slobbery lab kiss and Carol told me a little bit about the children we were going to see and the protocol. She then took me to the school psychologist's office and introduced me.

"Jean and her dog, Bella, will be joining us here every Tuesday. Bella hasn't worked in a school before, but she's good with children."

The psychologist asked me what made Bella a good therapy dog, and I told her she's sensitive and attentive. She reads people well. And she radiates happiness, like most dogs. She thanked me for joining them, and then Carol and I walked down the hall for Max's first appointment. Carol used to be an elementary school teacher and had just retired at the end of the previous school year. She was thrilled to have more time to invest in the program she started, and having been a teacher herself, she was diplomatic and understood their schedules.

She knocked softly on a classroom door, opened it a few feet, and asked the teacher if Mark was ready for his visit. The teacher nodded and reminded Mark, a cute second grade boy, to select a book to read to Max. Carol introduced me to Mark, but he had eyes for only Max, his right hand stroking the length of his back as we walked slowly down the hall.

We got into the Safe Room, a place for students to read, have quiet time, or meet one-on-one with their teachers. Carol told me never to close the door; we must be visible to others at all times. This was the world we lived in. Mark sat down on a thick gym mat on the floor and Max flopped down beside him. Carol sat on the other side of Max and asked Mark what he was going to read to Max. He held up a book about snakes.

"Good topic," said Carol. "I think Max will like that."

Max was fast asleep but it didn't matter; Mark pressed up against him. Reading a book to a dog was safe, fun, and free of judgment. Carol listened but didn't correct Mark when he mispronounced words. When the story was done, Carol asked Mark if he'd like to walk Max down the hallway. She clipped a second leash onto his collar and Mark proudly led Max down the hall to the front of the school. Other children saw him, some passing in the hallway, others from their classrooms. This was status, a top prize, not remedial reading. Being with the dog was the best. In the front lobby, Carol let go of the leash and gave Mark a tennis ball to throw gently for Max.

We walked Mark back to his classroom, and Carol told his teacher that he did a wonderful job reading the snake book. The other children wanted to pet Max, but Carol told them not now. Max was working.

Carol and I arranged to meet right outside the school the following week. I would have Bella with me, and we wanted the dogs to meet on neutral territory. I told Carol Bella was often afraid of large dogs and may not be friendly, and I thanked her for letting me see what Max did. "It's really inspiring," I told her, and meant it. On the forty-minute drive home, I thought about the children I saw and how a dog made them feel relaxed about reading. Accepted. Fine just as they were. These were children whom the teachers and school psychologist had identified as at risk. We didn't ask why, we didn't know the details, we just showed up with a dog and became friends. I liked this not-being-in-charge thing. I liked that dogs had a different way of being smart and still knew what to do. And I really liked the fact that we were not making judgments or handing out grades and that we had no authority. It was liberating.

As the youngest of three children, I was always behind and rushing to catch up, something I couldn't do no matter how hard I tried. I'd scream "Wait for me!" and my brother and sister would run so fast until I could no longer see them. And I'd stand there, gasping for breath, hating them for leaving me alone. School was like this, too, as being A-students seemed effortless to them, while I struggled to master subtraction and spelling. My second-grade teacher yelled at me for using my fingers, but I couldn't make sense of numbers in my head. So I believed I wasn't smart, and it wasn't until college that I finally had the confidence to know otherwise. Wouldn't it have been wonderful, when I was a child, to have had a dog as one of my teachers? To have had that companion, a creature who provided reassurance and acceptance, and who could have helped me figure out that although I was the youngest, I was smart in my own way, and would find a way to learn on my own terms when I was ready.

🐾 🐾

When Bella met Max, her hair shot up and she backed away. Max was big, but Carol had trained dogs for years and suggested we take a walk around the school parking lot. Bella relaxed, and by the time we walked into the school, she had snuck up behind Max to sniff him.

Now we were a pack of two women and two dogs. We took up a lot of space in the school hallway. I signed in, and as a class passed us on their way to the school library, the children squealed with delight. Their teacher kept them in line. We were to meet the three children I would start working with the following week. Carol wanted to make sure they would be okay with Bella.

As we opened each classroom door, the dogs were like magnets. They were beacons calling the children to them. Only the children we would be working with were allowed to get out of their seats and meet Bella. Bella was jazzed up. She liked it here. I think she liked the energy, the attention, maybe just the excitement of being in a school. This was her first time here and she acted as if she owned it. It was her domain. Maybe she liked small creatures because they didn't tower over her, or maybe these were the puppies she never had.

Carol made the introductions and told the children we would be back next week to meet with them. I could hardly wait. All three children were in first grade: Courtney, Justin, and Ely. Carol had written down their classroom numbers for me and when I was scheduled to see them. The following week, I saw Courtney first. She had long brown hair and sparkling eyes. Her teacher reminded her to pick out a few books to read to Bella and she did. Once we were out in the hallway, I told her I was glad to meet her. She only looked at Bella, clearly taken with her.

We sat down on the mats in the Safe Room, the door open, with Bella between us.

"What would you like to read first?"

She held up a book about a fawn.

"Sounds good. Bella and I will listen."

As she read about the fawn who had to stay still while her mother was gone, I noticed Courtney's left hand resting on the back of Bella's neck, her fingers under her fur. I silently rooted for the fawn, rooted for Courtney while she read.

"That was great!" I said when she finished the book. "Want to read one more and then you can play with Bella?"

She nodded.

The second book was about two small dogs who were afraid of a fox.

"Make sure you're listening," I told Bella, whose eyes were closed.

When she was done, I gave Courtney a tennis ball and asked her to hide it.

"Let's see how long it takes Bella to find it," I said.

Courtney put the ball behind a desk and when she told me it was okay, I let Bella go.

"Wow—three seconds."

We did this several times and then I attached a second leash to Bella's collar and Courtney helped walk Bella back to her classroom. Before we got back in, I told her I would see her next week. She smiled and skipped into her class. She reminded me of my daughter when she was this age—my first baby who was now in her late thirties.

Justin couldn't really read but made up words that were close to those on the page. Since I was not the teacher, I didn't correct him. He was obsessed with frogs, so we looked at the pictures, we talked about catching tadpoles, I found out all the places he'd been where there were frogs.

Ely had a worksheet to complete. He wrote his name in huge block letters and had to fill in the blanks in a story about turtles. I told him I was afraid of snapping turtles. He looked at me as if I had spoken a foreign language and went back to erasing most of what he'd written. Soon there would be a large hole in the paper. I saw how hard this was for him.

"Let's do one together," I suggested.

He nodded.

We got one sentence completed about turtle eggs, and then it was play time. I didn't want him to see his time with Bella as work. He asked if he could walk her down the long school hallway to the front door.

"Good idea. Let's do it."

He strutted as other kids passed him in the hallway.

"This is Bella," he said. "She's visiting me."

As I drove home, I thought about how different this experience had been. Bella was patient and relaxed. She seemed to do better here than in the rehab facility or hospital. Maybe it was a relief for her to be with people who weren't old or sick. Maybe some maternal instinct had kicked in. What was really neat was that, over time, we got to know these children well and they loved being with Bella. She didn't care what they did or how well they could spell. She just wanted to be with them, and they with her. It was a mutual admiration. It was simple. A dog and kids. A dog who helped them learn just by being there. I have always believed we need friends of different ages and species, and that these relationships ground us in joy. Tuesday was now my favorite day of the week, as I got to spend it with three first graders who couldn't wait to see Bella and me.

Chapter 22

FAVORITES CAN STILL BITE

Winter–Spring 2013
Stonington, Connecticut

I was finally not only a volunteer. For the past few months I'd been teaching my Boomers Back to Work! class, and I was loving it. I got to help older workers let go of their stereotypes about age. It was interactive, upbeat, and I loved seeing how hope was a huge motivator.

It wasn't easy, as some of the people in my class had been out of work a long time. On one occasion, when asked about goals for the class, a woman said, "I need a car." Another apologized to me for not attending the second part of the class as he had just been diagnosed with stage four pancreatic cancer. And although the economy had been slowly recovering from the recession of 2008, there didn't seem to be too many signs of hiring in this part of Connecticut. Like my volunteer work, I was faced with problems

I couldn't solve. But, unlike my volunteer work, I received a check in the mail after each class and it made me feel wonderful.

My teaching schedule was flexible so I rarely missed going to The Starfish Home or the Gales Ferry Elementary School. I liked this balance. There was always enough work, but never too much. I had time for friends, time to take long walks with Bob and Bella, time for our grandchildren. As Bob and I came up on our first anniversary of living in Connecticut, I realized I had created a diverse and satisfying lifestyle and fostered new friendships. Deb and I had grown close, Kat and I partnered well in our work in the hospital, and I was getting to know the staff as well as the residents at The Starfish Home.

The Resident Care Coordinator, Jan, had a small office catty-cornered from the nurse's station. She wore a white nursing uniform. Bella and Shelby knew she had a stash of dog treats in her desk drawer and quickly developed a routine. Whenever we walked past the nurse's station, they dragged us to her office, and Bella (and once in a while, Shelby) put her paws up on Jan's desk. They were both excited—they knew what was coming.

"Well, here you are!" said Jan, looking at the two dogs. "So nice of you to visit."

The tails wagged like crazy.

"Here you go, girls," said Jan, feeding Bella a treat and being careful of her fingers, as Shelby's enthusiasm made it difficult for her to know the difference between fingers and treats.

I took a photo with my cell phone and brought a printed copy to Jan the following week. Jan had been there twenty-eight years, and from our brief chats with her, Deb and I got the feeling that she loved the patients, loved making a difference at what for many was the end of their lives. Her own father had died there.

I wanted to ask her about Beverly but couldn't ask any direct questions. So instead I said, "Beverly seems to really enjoy our visits."

"That's good. She's been here a while."

"Oh?" I responded, fighting the urge to ask how long.

"In and out. Her husband took care of her until he died, then she had to be here permanently."

But does she have children and do they visit? I wanted to say.

From the way she treated her dolls, I was certain she was a mother, but it was odd to know so little, to know only what Beverly could tell me without words, on some days hiding under a pile of blankets, and other times grinning as I sang to her babies. I had worked as a corporate trainer and had lectured about body language, about the power of posture, gesture, voice, and facial expressions. But now, for the first time, it was all I had. It was like being in a foreign land with no guide book.

Deb and I thanked Jan for the treats and worked our way down the side hallway to Michael, who had a feeding tube and resented being there. It seemed to me that he was suffering more than many of the others because he was in pain and he was much younger and more aware. He was stuck there, but his medical condition required twenty-four hour nursing care.

He had two stashes in his room: dog treats on a shelf for Bella and Shelby (and the other dogs who visited), and chocolate bars in a cabinet beside his bed. So we got the box of dog treats and placed one in his left hand, being careful to say clear of his catheter and feeding tube.

"I like the dogs," he said, as they took the treats from his hand.

Then, because he had trained us well, we asked him if he wanted a piece of chocolate and we unwrapped a mini-bar for him. For that split second, while the dogs were chewing and the chocolate was dissolving in his mouth, everyone was happy. Then the tirade began: we heard what this nurse did wrong, how he couldn't get any help, and about why they stopped the hospice worker who used to come in and give him a massage every week. Now that he wasn't dying, he had to endure living.

We couldn't solve any of his problems, but we listened. We nodded. We sympathized. The dogs wondered if more treats would be offered and shifted their weight from leg to leg like people waiting for a train. We told him we would see him next week and we always said we enjoyed talking with him, but we knew we barely made a dent. He watched us leave the room and then turned his head back to the window where he could see cars going by, where he could see people leading the kind of busy lives he would never have.

When we ran into Bonnie, one of the RNs who was steering the drug cart down the hall, we were very careful not to sound critical of the staff. We simply relayed Michael's complaints and said, "He doesn't understand," and she replied, "I know." We thanked her and moved on to the hallway that led to the dining room.

Deb and I had developed our own shorthand language. It went something like this: "Nope," "Not today," "Sleeping," "Allergic," "Amputee (very afraid the dogs would bump into her)," "Maybe?" and "Yes." The amazing thing was that we almost never disagreed or read the residents differently. For the first four or five months, I was the follower, but now that I was comfortable here and had confidence in Bella's abilities, we worked as a team.

It was impossible even for the dogs not to have favorites, so as we headed down the hallway, Bella and Shelby passed by rooms where the patients were always asleep or very agitated, and headed for Alice and Jackie's, the jackpot of all treats. Alice's eyebrows shot up as we entered the room, and Nancy grinned ear to ear and announced "The doggies are here!" Deb and I loved her. Bella decided to get a head start and jumped onto Jackie's bed.

"Oh," said Jackie. "She—she wants to see me."

"Yes, she does," I replied, keeping my hand on Bella's leash so she didn't overpower Jackie.

Shelby came up to the bed as if to say, "Hey, don't forget I'm here too."

Nancy waited for Jackie to give both dogs treats, and then she brought her stash out of her large handbag. Alice got a bit lost in the excitement, but since she had a toy cat on her lap, I asked her about the cat.

Eyebrows shot up again. So I tried something. "Meow," I said.

Nothing, so I tried it again.

"Meow," she answered, sounding exactly like a cat.

Back and forth we went, having a great time, until Bella and Shelby started to bark.

"Whoops," I said, "guess we fooled the dogs."

Nancy laughed, happy that her mother was having fun. I had learned that Alice had not been an easy mother. She was a mother who even now lashed out. I was amazed by Nancy's heart, that she could overlook the past, not ask much of the present, and week after week, take such good care of her mother. She did her nails, brought in flowers for her to arrange, made sure she was dressed with matching scarves and earrings, and monitored all her care. Nancy had become the mother she wished she had.

"I love you guys," she told Bella and Shelby as we were leaving. And they loved her, not just because of the treats, but I'm sure because they knew how she felt about them. "Why don't you doggies stay with me?" she asked, knowing she'd get a reaction out of Deb and me.

"No way!" Deb said, "this is my girl." She had another dog, but she and Shelby were bonded in a special way, and no one would ever get between them.

Several months later when I visited the rehab facility without Deb and Shelby, I walked into Alice and Jackie's room, smiling. I knew this would be the high point of the afternoon, but Alice took one look at me and shouted, "Damn you!" I recoiled as though I had been slapped in the face. Nancy looked like she was sinking through the floor.

"Oh, Alice," I said, making light of her anger, but she glared at me. Today I was the enemy.

"Damn you to hell!"

I was stuck, frozen. There was pure hatred in her eyes.

"Mom!" said Nancy.

Alice ignored her.

"It's just me, Alice," I said, trying to get over the shock.

"You, you—you're" and she rattled off a string of curses.

It's just the disease, I told myself, looking away, moving across the room to Jackie's bed.

After she'd given Bella a treat and I sat down on the edge of her bed, she told me, "Something isn't right."

I waited.

"Not right. Not working. My brain. It hurts."

"Oh, Jackie," I said, "I'm sorry."

"I can't make it, it won't, and I can't, you know—"

Her voice trailed off and in her face was confusion, sorrow, anger, and despair.

I put my hand on her arm. Bella had curled up on her bed and was taking a quick nap. Nancy, who was one of the most compassionate people I had ever met, looked at Jackie with tears in her eyes.

"And the doctor, he won't because of the other thing, so I'm still here."

"Yes," I said, "you are."

157

Her hand stroked Bella's smooth back, resting on her short fur, and I knew she was doing a better job than I was of comforting Jackie.

"I like this thing," she said.

"Her harness?" I asked.

A nod, and I was thinking how terrifying it must be not to be able to find the words, the right words, for things. A few weeks later, we found out that her family had moved her to another facility because, after twenty years in this place, she had come to the end of her rope. She was done.

Bella and I visited her once in the new facility and she knew who we were, but without Nancy as well as Shelby and Deb, it wasn't the same. It was sad, and even Bella's presence couldn't change that. The light had gone from her eyes.

Chapter 23

WHAT WE DO

Spring 2013
Stonington, Connecticut

It was difficult to explain to others what we did and why we had come to love the nursing home, or rehab facility, as it was called. It was easy to think of it as a dumping ground, a place to put Grandma, or Mom, or an older sibling when he or she could no longer be managed at home. It could be seen as the only alternative when a family member became ill and needed constant care. For some, it was a temporary solution after surgery, usually joint replacement, as it wasn't safe to live alone until they recovered. I used to be afraid of these facilities and assumed that most residents were so out of it there was no point in trying to connect. When I had visited my aunt or a neighbor in a similar place, I dashed in, got to their rooms as quickly as I could, and got out. It was a gauntlet where the empty stares and nonsense words were dangers I had to outrun.

But being here week after week with Deb and the dogs changed that. It was finally spring and we had been coming here together for a year. We had a sense of ownership about this facility. It was ours—ours and the dogs. We knew everyone's name (with the help of the name plaques outside each room). We knew the staff, we were familiar with the routines, and of course we knew who welcomed the dogs, who was stashing Cheerios, or crackers, or dog treats, and who would rather say a quick hello to the dogs than to us.

"Oh, look, here they are," was what many residents said as we entered their rooms.

And Bella and Shelby, tails wagging, sashayed in, ambassadors of exuberance. They didn't mind the awful smells, the sticky floors, or the garbled sounds that some of the residents made, or if they did, they didn't show it. It didn't matter to them that most patients couldn't remember their names, or if they were sisters, or what breed they were. Their power was immediate. Dog equals joy. Dog brings life. Nothing beats dog.

Deb and I made an interesting mistake once. We called one woman Lois although her name was Jane. Neither of us knew how this started, but since Lois (really Jane) was deaf, she didn't mind what we called her as long as the dogs were there. And she discovered that they loved Cheerios. She poured the cereal into a little ceramic basket that she kept on her bedside table and fed Cheerios to Bella and Shelby, letting her hand get slobbered, laughing the whole time.

We came to love the Cheery Cheerio Lady, as Deb called her, and the dogs did too. Her room was in the first hallway we went down, so we started our visits looking forward to seeing her. On good days, she waited in her wheelchair just outside her room with the ceramic basket in her hands. But one day in April, when spring was really here for good, Deb met me in the parking lot and told me she had died. Lois had died.

I had seen her the week before and she'd been agitated, lying in bed. I asked her, "Lois, can I get you anything?" and she had asked for a ginger ale. I told her I'd be right back and went to the refrigerator near the nurses' station to get her a cold can of ginger ale and a straw.

"Thank you," she said. "I sometimes feel very alone here. You are so kind."

I sat on the edge of her bed, Bella watching me, and spent about five minutes with her. After I left, we passed the nurses' station and I mentioned to Bonnie that she had seemed upset.

"She's got an infection," she told me, "but we're taking care of it."

I told Deb I didn't want to walk past her room because it would seem so empty without her.

"I know," said Deb. "But we've got to see her roommate. She likes the dogs, too."

I nodded and followed her through the front door. As we turned into Lois's room, the lights were off and it was hard to see. I assumed that Lois's bed was empty so I looked to the far side of the room where her roommate was. But something moved in the empty bed and Deb screamed, "She's alive!"

I stepped back as if hit by an electrical current. There was Lois, just waking up from a nap, smiling at us.

"Oh, my God!" I said.

"Not dead," Deb whispered.

"Hi girls," said Lois, really Jane. This was what she always said as she didn't remember either our names or the dogs'.

"Oh, hi," said Deb, stuttering. "Dogs are here."

"Nice to see you," I added, my eyes wide.

The dogs circled around her knees for the Cheerio-feeding routine. I couldn't look at Deb because if I did, I'd lose it.

"How have you been?" I asked. "Better than last week?"

She nodded, interested in us, but obsessed with the dogs. They were her children.

After we said goodbye and were out in the hall, we collapsed with laughter.

"Your face!" I told Deb. "Oh, that was something."

"Yeah, well, you looked as if you'd seen a ghost."

And then more giggles, more gasping for air. In this place where death was everywhere, Lois had beaten the odds. The dogs looked at us and wondered why we'd stopped in the middle of the hallway. We carefully read the name plate and saw that this was indeed Jane, not Lois.

"She's been resurrected," said Deb.

"Oh, God," I said. "This was better than Lazarus."

When we got to Jan's office, we asked her who died and it was indeed a woman named Lois, but our friend, our Cheery Cheerio Lady was Jane. Deb and I laughed every time we looked at each other. We barely held it together, and when we were out in the parking lot, we had tears streaming down our faces. I couldn't remember the last time I'd laughed like this. It made me feel as though I were ten years old, exploding with giggles.

When Deb got home, she sent an email to the minister of our church so that he knew we had witnessed a resurrection and that life everlasting was alive and well at the rehab facility.

My relationship with Beverly continued, and when we finally got one of those warm spring days where everything felt new and fresh, I asked an aide if I could take Beverly outside onto the terrace.

"As long as you stay with her and bring her back in, it's fine."

I had no idea if she'd like this, but I was hoping that fresh air and a little sunshine might seep through the gloom that surrounded her. I knelt down by her chair while Deb and Shelby visited other residents and told her that we were going to go outside. Nothing. I patted her arm and said I was glad to see her. More nothing.

I unlocked the brakes on her wheelchair and moved her very slowly to the door. Bella followed. I propped the door open with a brick and got her out into the dappled shade. I pulled up a chair beside her and waited. She sat there. Bella sniffed around and looked at me as if wondering what to do now.

"Feel the breeze?" I said to her.

A dull stare.

"Does your baby like it out here?"

She rocked the doll up and down.

"You're such a good Mommy."

I hummed a lullaby and was rewarded with a shy smile. A flicker.

Then I told myself to be quiet. To just be here. We watched as the wind made the tree branches sway and our hair lift and fall. Just like the doll. Up and down.

Hush.

Don't worry, I am holding you tight and will never let you go.

🐾 🐾

Kat and I, plus Boo and Bella, were up on the fourth floor in the hospital in New London. I went into the first room while she chatted with a nurse at the desk. There was a frail, elderly man in bed, and his face lit up when he saw Bella. I asked him if he'd like Bella to put her paws up so that she could be closer to him, and he nodded and gave her a few treats.

After several minutes, I said, "Nice to meet you," and left. Kat and Boo went into his room while I worked my way down the hall. I was almost done with this ward when I saw a young woman, lying in her bed, crying. My first thought was not to bother her, but her mother, who was sitting next to the bed, said, "Please come visit. We'd love to see the dog."

"You sure?" I asked, and she nodded. "This is Bella."

The young woman continued to cry, but I could see she was distracted by Bella.

"Would you like her to come up on the bed and lie down next to you?" I asked.

She nodded, and once Bella was in place, I watched her hand stroke Bella's back and chest. Even her head.

She stopped crying and I told her that Bella was a therapy dog and that we came here every week.

Her mother said, "We just found out that she has a brain tumor—but it's very small. They caught it early."

"Oh, my," I said.

"They're going to dissolve it with chemo," her mother told me.

I looked at this young woman and saw that Bella's quiet, warm presence had taken the edge off her fear.

She looked up at me and said, "I just had a baby a week ago."

I didn't know what to say. This seemed like too much, so I simply asked, "Is the baby all right?"

"Yes, she's fine," and a tentative smile transformed her face wet from tears, eyes red and puffy.

The phone next to the bed rang and the mother answered it. She repeated the basic information she had told me and hung up.

"That was Aunt Josie," she told her daughter. "She's hysterical and wants to see you."

"No," said the daughter, her hand resting on Bella's side.

The mother didn't argue, and I thought that her family meant well, but what she needed right now was what Bella was giving her: nonverbal reassurance, comfort, and hope. No drama. I'd often thought of Bella as a bridge—a way for patients to get from here to there—but now I saw that she was more of a catalyst. She changed the chemistry, the essence of how they felt, because she was a dog, because she knew what to do, because she snuck under their defenses and touched their hearts.

Chapter 24

INVITATIONS

Late Spring 2013
Stonington, Connecticut

I t was wonderful to be wanted. To be asked for. A young woman visiting her aunt at the rehab facility told us she worked for the Cerebral Palsy Foundation and wanted to know if we'd consider visiting. Deb looked at me and we both nodded. Sure, why not? We were so confident in our dogs' abilities that we rarely said no. We arranged a date and time, and Deb and I, who hadn't quite yet been brave enough to carpool with the dogs, met in the parking lot of the foundation.

It was a hot, late spring day, and we gave the dogs time to stretch their legs and sniff the grass. As we entered the lobby, we saw a young woman strapped into a wheelchair, banging her head repeatedly against the head rest. *Thump, thump, thump.*

Bella looked up at me as if asking if this was okay.

"Hi," said Deb. "Would you like to see the dogs?"

Thump, thump, thump.

"Bella, put your paws up." I pointed to the tray attached to the wheelchair and Bella put her front paws up and gazed at this girl. There was a momentary silence, then more thumping. I said quietly, "She's glad to see you."

Our contact at this facility greeted us and asked if we'd like to start in the activity room. We followed her into a room that was crowded with wheelchairs. A few aides stood in the room, but it was mostly teenagers—young people—strapped into their chairs. The dogs were a surprise. The sounds in the room intensified. There was grunting, some words we could understand, and many we couldn't. Two girls flung back on a couch as if hurled there by a powerful wind.

I glanced at Deb and her eyebrows shot up. Shelby was unstoppable, always calm, and never bothered by too much noise or stimulation. The same could not be said for Bella. She was on alert, unsure.

"It's okay, girl," I told her, slipping a treat into her mouth. I needed her to stay focused on the job, on reaching out to these kids.

I bent close to a boy who looked to be about twelve, bent over sideways so it was hard to see his face. "This is Bella," I said, "and she's come to visit you."

"Bella" he said.

"Yes, that's right. That's her name. Want to give her a treat?"

I suddenly realized he couldn't open or untwist his fingers.

"Is it okay if I put the treat on top of your hand?"

I got a little nod, and Bella very gently took the treat and ate it.

"Oh," I said. "She liked that. Thank you so much."

His head went to the other side and I had a sudden image of his parents, of the huge task of taking care of him. And then I thought of all the things he may never be able to do: ride a bike, go for a walk, swim, have a girlfriend, get married, be a father, work. This seemed so wrong.

I didn't have time in this crowded room to let sadness envelop me or to ask the unanswerable question: why? I simply patted his arm, told him it was nice to meet him, and followed Deb and Shelby around the room. Nothing stopped either of them. Nothing beat their unflappable goodness.

We were then led through a long hallway into a room that was used for physical therapy. Only the therapist was there, but in two seconds she was on the floor, petting both dogs. Bella licked her face and Shelby wagged her tail, her broad back swaying.

Then we went into a large room with even more wheelchairs and some patients lying on mats on the floor. One girl on the floor was swinging a plastic baseball bat around. I kept Bella far from her. Others were being fed. I stopped by the chair of a boy with a baseball cap on. "You a Red Sox fan?" I asked.

I saw a wonderful twinkle in his eyes, and he nodded.

I told him that Bella was obsessed with balls—mostly tennis balls—and that she could run like the wind and catch them as far as you can throw them. I asked him if I could put one of her treats on his tray and he nodded. Bella put her paws up and grabbed the treat. He made a sound that could've been "Yeah!"

I liked that this boy seemed so energetic. So I told him Bella's story: how she was rescued off a beach in Puerto Rico as a small puppy, taken care of there, and then flown to Newark airport along with forty other dogs.

"Can you imagine the noise?" I asked him, and he smiled.

"And can you imagine how scared those puppies were in the cargo hold of a jet?"

He looked at me, mesmerized.

"Then she was taken to a shelter in New Jersey and she had to have all her shots and be neutered. My husband and I got her when she just four months old. And she was crazy! She chased the cat, ate my sandal, and was difficult to train. But after lots of practice, we did it."

He did his best to clap his hands. This was the best audience we had ever had. I knew the room was full of other children, but I couldn't walk away. I wanted to stay here where I had a connection, a friend. Bella looked at me and waited. Deb and Shelby were on the other side of the room. I looked into this boy's brown eyes and saw such tenderness and composure. How did he do it, locked in this broken body?

"We really enjoyed meeting you," I said, getting ready at last to walk away.

"Bella," he said. And I wanted to cry.

I never forgot that taking care of Bella and watching out for her safety was my number-one priority. If a situation wasn't good for her, it was my job to get her out of there. I was still thinking about the boy we just saw when I realized we were too close to the girl swinging the baseball bat. We quickly walked around her and didn't try to interact or include her. It may have seemed unfair, but it was the foundation of what all therapy dog teams did—keep the dog safe. Don't overwhelm them. Pay attention to what they can and can't do. Respect their boundaries.

In the last room, children were being fed. I couldn't make out what the food was except that it was mushy and something easy to swallow. This was another layer of sadness. These kids couldn't eat a peanut butter and jelly sandwich. They couldn't hold an ice cream cone or a cookie. I suddenly remembered a boy from my childhood. We went from kindergarten to twelfth grade together, and at a reunion, maybe fifteen years after we had graduated from high school, he said to me, "You have no idea what having a special needs child does to you."

I had looked at him then, wondering if he was being dramatic. Wondering why he was telling me this.

"I guess you're right," I had answered, not sure what else to say.

"Or to a marriage," he added.

I looked at his face then, remembering him at school, seeing in my mind the way he was always making practical jokes and laughing. He wasn't laughing now. He was tired.

"I'm sorry," I said, and he walked off. That was the last time I saw him. He didn't come to any other reunions.

I get it now, I thought, then corrected myself: No, that wasn't right. I didn't get it. I didn't have a child with needs like these kids. But I got it from the outside. I got it because Bella had led me here. I was given a glimpse into this world because of my dog.

Deb and I lasted about forty-five minutes. Then it was time to leave. The woman thanked us and invited us back. She told us that the dogs were a hit. We said we would return, but I wasn't sure we would. Part of it was that we were busy and already committed at other places. And part of it was that this was too hard. We went where the balance was right—where what we gave and what we got were in a reciprocal, healthy relationship. That wasn't selfish, it was smart. We had working dogs, and just like people, the work had to fit.

Out in the hot sun in the parking lot, we gave the dogs water and let them sniff around in the grass. I didn't have to say anything to Deb, as I saw in her face the same stunned sadness. But then I told her, "I'm glad we came."

She looked at me, hugged Shelby, and said, "Yeah, me too."

Colleges also asked for therapy dogs around exam time to reduce student stress. And sometimes they were asked to be part of a health fair since the dogs helped students feel balanced and connected. Kat Bishop knew every dog-related organization in the area and sent out an email to see which therapy dog teams could go to Connecticut College for the health fair. I signed up, wondering how Bella would do with a crowd of students and other dogs.

We found the right building on campus and walked into a large gymnasium set up with tables, balloons, food, and clumps of students around the dogs who were already there.

"Easy now, girl," I told Bella as we settled into a place near the other dogs, but far enough away that Bella could stay relaxed. A freshman boy walked up and asked if he could pet her.

"Sure," I said. "This is Bella and she's a bit head-shy so pet her on the back."

Bella moved so that he couldn't reach her.

"Do you mind sitting or squatting? She gets nervous when people stand over her."

"Oh sure," said the student, and he plopped himself down. Bella changed into a different dog and licked him on the face.

"Well, you're friendly, aren't you?" he asked Bella. She circled around him, claiming him as her own with friendly pokes of her snout.

"Hey," said another student, bending down quickly to pet Bella. She ducked. I thought to myself, *This is going to be a long morning*.

The first student told the second one to sit down, so he did. Now Bella had two puppies of her own and was fine. The first boy told me he was from New York City and never had a dog. The second grew up in Connecticut and missed his dog at home. I asked them if it was hard to adjust to college, remembering my first winter a thousand miles from home.

"Yeah, kinda," said the first student.

"Not bad," said the other. "But I go home some weekends."

I nodded, thinking back to my freshman year and how lost I felt, how unsure I was of being able to succeed at college. A dog could have helped. I didn't tell these boys we didn't have cell phones in those days and that long-distance calls home were too expensive and could be made only for an emergency. So we wrote letters two or three times a week. And it cost too much to come home for Thanksgiving, so I had to make it from late August until Christmas break. That was an eternity.

What would really blow their minds was that I didn't even visit my college before attending. My parents drove me to the airport in New York and put me on a charter plane. I sat next to a girl from the city who ate a large salami during most of the flight. And because I had been brought up properly, I had on a suit, stockings, and heels. I was a college girl. I was a woman of the world, when in reality I was a very young, scared, seventeen-year-old kid who had grown up in the middle of nowhere and had no idea what she was doing.

The boys left and some girls appeared, saying in high-pitched voices, "Oh, look how cute she is!" And my maternal pride kicked right in as if I had something to do with it. "Yes, she is."

After they left, the head of the psychology department introduced herself and thanked me for participating. She gave Bella a stuffed animal and a bag of treats. I got a button that said, laugh more. I put it on my sweater and couldn't wait to see Bob's face when he saw it. He'd have an ironic comment to make about laughter on demand.

We met some of the other therapy dog teams, and Bella did well. Because I'd worked extensively as a career coach, I thought of Bella adding this credential to her résumé as though she had to look for work: *Participated in student health fair and helped comfort freshmen students.*

Nothing made me prouder than saying she was a working dog. And that went for me, too. I was a working girl, both volunteer and paid. I was teaching my Boomer class and still doing occasional jobs for my former company. But most exciting of all, we were out there in our community, building bonds with nursing home residents, hospital patients, school children, and now college students. Bella and I were blessed to have jobs we loved.

"Want to go home?" I asked, and she was ready. She bit the leash and played tug of war on our way out the door. It was her way of being done, of releasing her pent-up energy and the stress of being well-behaved.

Two other colleges asked for dogs. One was a large university in Rhode Island where Bob got his undergraduate degree. He came with me, as he knew the campus. After we parked the car, we walked Bella over to a large central lawn crowded with hundreds of students.

"Oh no," I said, already knowing this would be overwhelming for Bella.

Just as we approached the crowd, Bella started to squeal in pleasure. She saw Kat, Wren, and Boo, and hurled herself at the two dogs, nearly knocking them over.

Kat laughed and the students were amused. "Well, look at you," she said, trying to keep Bella from getting tangled in her two leashes.

Bob helped me get her away from Wren and Boo, who were clearly stars of the show. Their coats were beautiful, multicolored, sleek invitations to be touched, and they weren't bothered by the noise and excitement of all these students.

Bob and I spread out a blanket on the ground a bit farther back from the center of this whirlwind and encouraged students to kneel or sit next to her. It didn't work. She was too nervous, too wired by all the activity. We lasted about fifteen minutes and walked back to the car. I was at war with myself, wanting her to be like Wren and Boo while realizing that wasn't who she was. She was not easy, not relaxed, not an I-love-everybody kind of dog.

On the long ride home, I gave myself a lecture on acceptance. On different gifts. Just because Bella wasn't good at this kind of college fair didn't mean she didn't do other things well. I had to let go of what she wasn't. A few weeks later, we went to another college during exam week. It was a beautiful, small campus overlooking the water. Bob and I had walked Bella here in the past so she was comfortable and relaxed. When we got to the student center, we found a quiet spot and several students came over to visit with her. I asked them about their studies, but their focus was on Bella.

The girls said, "Oh, look at that face!" The boys, less verbally exuberant, got down on the floor and gave her treats. One boy told us there was free ice cream during exam week and showed me where it was. Bella and I each got a small cup of vanilla, and she thought this was a fine way to end our visit. I realized as we walked across the lawn in the spring air filled with the smell of salt water, that I would never be lonely or bored as long as I had a therapy dog. The doors kept opening.

Chapter 25

BEVERLY'S BLESSING

Summer 2013
Stonington, Connecticut

Deb and I met as usual outside The Starfish Home with our dogs. She was excited, as her daughter had just gotten engaged, but was a bit overwhelmed with all the decisions that had to be made. I was feeling a bit giddy as it had finally occurred to me that keeping the door open with my former company was not good for my health. And I had found a good way to do it—a good way to end the tense meetings with people who had just been let go. I simply asked for more money—more in line with what I had been earning—and they never called again.

We got into the rehab facility and after visiting with two residents, Deb turned to me and asked, "Is there a full moon?"

I burst out laughing and told her that it would be full in about two days.

"That explains it," she said. "Is it me or is everyone a little more out-there than usual?"

"It's you," I said, and we laughed.

Bella and Shelby caught our giggly mood and competed in a friendly way to see who could get more treats. Bella pulled out her trump card and jumped up on a resident's bed while Shelby, who was considerably bigger than Bella, got right up against another resident's legs and let her pet her on the head. So there!

When we arrived at Starfish the following week, an aide was waiting for us in the lobby. She briefed us about new patients and which ones were likely to want to see the dogs. She told us when someone was too ill to see them, or when a patient had been moved to the hospital or had died.

"Hey," said Deb, as she put Shelby's harness on.

The aide leaned down and told both Shelby and Bella that she was glad to see them.

"I've got to tell you something," she said, looking at Deb.

We froze.

"Wendy died this week."

Deb couldn't talk or move. She just stood there.

"I know you had a special bond," added the aide.

I put my hand on Deb's shoulder. "She really loved you and Shelby."

Deb nodded, still unable to say anything. Wendy was only in her forties, and although she had Down's syndrome, she still seemed young and vibrant. There were no warning signs that we noticed, no clear decline. One week she was there and the next, she wasn't. It was too much to take in. The dogs waited quietly, but when it was time to start visiting, Deb, her voice almost a whisper, thanked the aide for telling us. The aide patted her shoulder. Shelby looked up expectantly. We avoided Wendy's room and talked about the other residents instead. Deb soldiered on. She and Shelby were there for everyone, but for many weeks both of us expected to see Wendy being pushed down the hallway by her aide, her wide smile breaking through all the sadness when she caught sight of Shelby and Deb.

🐾 🐾

As we continued down the hallway, Deb said to me, "Isn't it funny how certain patients bond with us?" And she was right. There was magic that we couldn't control or explain. As if on cue, we saw Beverly walking very slowly down the hall, leaning on her walker, an aide at her side. The aide used one hand to hold the "baby" in front of Beverly as incentive. We had never seen Beverly walk.

"I know you're going to visit with your girl," said Deb. "Shelby and I will go see Karen."

I nodded, still dumbfounded that Beverly could walk. The aide got her into the dining room and helped her sit down in a chair.

"Here's your baby," she said, and Beverly clutched the doll to her chest.

I sat down in a chair next to hers and said, "Hi, Beverly."

There was a short hesitation, a moment when she wasn't sure who I was, but then she knew me. I got the first of a few shy smiles. I told her I'd missed her. I complemented her on the beautiful doll, and then I asked her if she'd like to give Bella a treat.

No reaction, just a blank stare.

The aide watched and I could see in her eyes that she thought Beverly wouldn't do it.

I took Beverly's hand and slowly lowered it to Bella's level. So far so good. Then I put a treat on her palm and saw her eyes open wide as she felt the soft fur of Bella's chin on her hand and the lick of her tongue.

I let go of her hand, told her "You did it!" and clapped my hands.

Beverly clapped, too, grinning with pleasure.

The aide looked at me and said, "Wow. I never saw her react to anything that much."

"It's taken time," I told her. More than a year of weekly visits.

And it had also taken love. I didn't say that, but I bet she saw it in my face.

After the aide left, Beverly took hold of my hand. Then I felt the tiniest rocking motion, a slow back and forth. My hand was a baby.

In that split moment—in that mother-and-child bond—my own mother was present. She was intertwined with both of us and my eyes filled with tears. She had been dead for thirteen years, and although I thought of her often, I didn't feel her presence. She was gone. But today, as a gift from Beverly, she was somehow here again.

The rules required that we didn't ask questions about anyone's condition, or how long they'd been there, or even if they had family. We only asked, "Would you like to see the dogs?" and then, if it was a yes, we asked how they were doing, or chatted about the weather, or for the ones who could talk, answered questions about the dogs.

Deb and I were both proud that our dogs were "rescues." It didn't mean they were rescuing anyone, although there were moments when I thought they came close. But rather, this one word conveyed they had a rough beginning and could have easily starved to death, been abused, or put down in a high-kill shelter. It also meant in many cases that the dog wasn't purebred. Although some breeds, like Greyhounds, had their own rescue leagues of purebred dogs that were retired from the racetrack.

For the patients who could talk and understand, the message they got was: here was a dog who was lost, then found, and who was now giving back. This was a grateful animal, one whose life was transformed and who now helped others. So, lucky was one part of it, and the other part was training and hard work.

The lesson I was learning, after a little more than a year there, was that I didn't own any of it. If I came in hoping that Beverly would smile at me or clap her hands, she wouldn't. If I expected that Joyce would share her shy grin and talk about the book she was reading (while hiding her left hand that had been crippled by a stroke), she wouldn't. If I hoped to be rewarded by some feeling of fulfillment, it wouldn't happen. And while I loved feeling appreciated, I knew now that I had to leave that at the door. It didn't belong here.

So it came down to showing up, listening, being present, and showing concern. In other words, Deb and I learned to be dogs. We didn't have agendas, or we tried not to. We were simply here and we took what happened in stride. One patient who had loved to see the dogs refused to see them after her leg was amputated, afraid they'd bump into her. Afraid of too much commotion. So we waved as we went by her room.

Chuck, another resident who had been crazy about dogs, the one Bella had decided needed her in his lap, stopped looking at them, and after a while stopped looking at us. And then he died. Although he was no longer there, we saw him every time we passed his room. We saw him and remembered the time I gave him a treat to give Bella, and before we could stop him, he popped it in his mouth.

Another resident self-published a book about her life. Deb called her "our resident author." She held up the book, tangible proof that she used to be something else, someone articulate with a full life. With something to say. Now she grinned at us and bit by bit was slipping away.

Sometimes, when we couldn't remember a patient's name, Deb said, "They've got our room ready, Jean." And we'd made a pact that when and if the time came and we'd have to be put in a rehab facility, we'd be roommates.

From our weekly visits, we learned about loss. I thought of that wonderful Dylan Thomas poem, "Do Not Go Gentle into That Good Night." And for sure there were the fighters. But others, like Olive, who was as dainty and frail as a good English tea cup, waited patiently. They took the setbacks in stride. They didn't seem afraid. They disappeared gradually, and always thanked us for coming in, often adding, "It's so nice of you."

This made me think of all that we were not: not nurses, not aides, not family, not doctors, not dietitians, not administrators. But that was part of the magic—we were extra, unnecessary, different, and we had a singular purpose: to bring joy and comfort. To be here.

The dogs strutted down the long hallways, past the carts with drawers full of medications, past the shelves of adult diapers, past the smells that gagged us, past the aides rushing back and forth with clean bedding, and Deb and I looked at each other and didn't have to say a word. We knew why we were here and, being together, the two of us and our dogs, the loss rarely overwhelmed us.

Chapter 26

EVERY DOG HAS A STORY

Summer–Fall 2013
Stonington, Connecticut

The bond we had with our own dogs was lasting and unbreakable. At The Starfish Home, a patient named Frank told me about a collie he had as a boy. His words fell over each other but I got the important parts of the story: there was a huge field behind his house, and he and this dog played there together. They were friends. They were inseparable. Frank could see this dog now and feel his fur. Because Bella was present, his dog was, too.

Frank collected newspaper articles. He loved history. He had a poster of the hurricane of 1938 on his wall. His bookcase was overflowing. He was like a librarian, always searching for information. And he loved to talk.

I'm not a patient person, but I did my best to listen, nod, and make encouraging noises. But if he was asleep or turned from the door, I sometimes passed by his room, as visiting with him was a commitment. It took time. And it was very difficult to leave. His idea of a visit was not five minutes and a little chat. He had things to say and needed someone to say them to.

As I looked at him, I realized he must have been a handsome man. He had a broad forehead, sandy hair, and still had some muscle tone. But the giveaway was his pants—gray sweatpants bunched up over his adult diaper with food stains from his chest down to his knees. He and his memory were in a life and death battle. Words, faces, even his own past was slipping away, often just out of reach. He stopped in the middle of a sentence and I waited. Bella looked at me as if to say *shouldn't we keep going?*

"Good girl," I told her while Frank struggled.

He used finding things as a way to cover up his memory loss.

"Oh, just a minute, just a minute!" And he turned his wheelchair around to face his bed, which was covered in newspaper articles.

Then he shuffled through them, held one close to his face so he could read it, and said, "See this?"

I didn't have my glasses on so I couldn't read.

"What about it?" I asked, trying to sound friendly while wondering how I could get out of his room.

"These politicians," he said. "They don't know what they're doing."

I nodded.

"And then they go and ruin things."

"That certainly can be true," I agreed.

"But never the way you expect."

Now I was stumped and decided to go for it.

"Hey, Frank. It was great to see you and we'll stop by next week. Okay?"

And before he could find another article, before he could trap me in another sentence that had no end, I waved and disappeared down the hall.

According to Deb, my "boyfriend" lived across the hall from Frank. His name was Bob (just like my husband) and he was a tiny man with long, delicate fingers. His hair was always neatly combed to one side. He had one of those things on his bed that looked like a tent that kept the blankets from pressing down on his feet, and he always wore a blue plaid bathrobe. His pants were neatly folded on the chair next to his bed. No clutter there.

Deb called him my "boyfriend" because he didn't give her the time of day when she visited without me. He was almost as talkative as Frank and loved to tell me about his dog, a German shepherd mix who only liked him.

"We lived in a small apartment in Queens and this dog wouldn't let anyone in unless I told him to sit in the corner. But then he'd stare at whoever had come to visit—not a friendly stare either!" Bob laughed.

It was hard to imagine him as young, but I knew he had been married (his wife died many years ago) and they had two grown children.

"He was guarding you," I said, and got immediate approval from Bob.

"Oh, yes. I had a cousin who liked to horse around, play practical jokes. That kind of thing. Couldn't do it around my dog. But once, he had the dumb idea to walk around the house and come in the back door. I was sitting in the kitchen and I saw my dog's head lift, ears erect, and watched as his whole body went on high alert."

I imagined that this dumb cousin was taught a lesson.

"Of course I don't know that it's my cousin, but I hear footsteps outside and the dog runs to the back door and lunges at it."

"Oh, God."

"Lucky for my stupid cousin, I get to the door before the dog breaks it down and attacks him."

Bob was having so much fun telling me this story, he could hardly contain himself.

"Boy, did I give it to him. And get this. He was ticked off that the dog came after him."

"Bet he never did that again."

Bob nodded, still far away. Still seeing that dog. Full of pride as if he had somehow made his dog into this ferocious and loyal creature.

"My wife and I cried for a week when he died and we never got another dog. Just couldn't do it, but I never felt as safe again. That was some dog."

Bella put her front paws up on Bob's bed. He extended his long fingers and I placed a treat on his palm. We'd gotten this down to a routine. Somehow from telling me about his dog, he veered off into a story about his two sisters. One died at four months old, and shortly after that, the older one became gravely ill.

"At first it seemed like a cold, but then she had trouble breathing and the doctor was useless. So my grandmother came over and sliced up a large onion, wrapped it in a dish towel, and put it on her chest. And you know what?"

I didn't know but could imagine the smell. The smell and the fear. "What?"

"In the morning she was better. Still weak, but better. We knew she would make it and the onions were all black. They had sucked the illness out of her."

"Really?"

Bob nodded.

"Amazing," I said. Bella nudged my leg as though I'd forgotten I was supposed to move on.

Bob's face was glowing as he remembered his sister. The one who made it. And the dog.

Deb was halfway down the hallway. I'd spent so much time with Frank and now Bob.

"See you next week, okay?" I asked, still wondering about the onions.

"Long as I'm here," said Bob with a flirtatious grin.

I guess he really was my boyfriend. He reminded me of an elf. His roommate was slumped over, fast asleep in his chair, so I skipped him. Bella pranced, so glad to get going and be back with Shelby.

I thought of the hospital as the place I went with Kat and her dogs, Wren or Boo. They were beautiful and well-trained. Kat was instrumental in getting this program launched a number of years earlier. As we got to know each other, I appreciated her quiet strength. She didn't draw attention to herself, but with one of her dogs, she glided into the patients' rooms, and with her soft voice and careful listening, they turned to her, trusted her, and shared their stories.

On one of our visits together, we visited a man she knew from her neighborhood. A farmer. He was strong and tan and reached hungrily for Wren. He recently had his leg amputated and told Kat he wasn't sure how he was going to get his chores done. Bella and I watched, and I was stunned by how matter-of-fact this man was. How calm. Kat was great with him: attentive, curious, and totally there. He asked to meet Bella and we walked over. Wren moved aside.

"Who's this little cutie?" he asked, scratching her behind the ears.

"This is Bella. We've been coming here for a year, mostly with Kat."

"You don't have much fur, do you?" He laughed.

"No, she's sleek but you'd be amazed by how much she sheds."

He reached to touch Bella on the head and she ducked. His eyebrows shot up and he asked, "Is she afraid? Does she have issues?"

I nodded, wondering if he'd like to hear the whole list: thunder, gun shots, having her head touched, sometimes men with hats, large dogs, small dogs, fireworks, nurses who came up to her too fast, wind, a door slamming, and so on.

"She's funny about having her head touched. Sometimes it's okay, but most of the time, even with my husband and me, she avoids it. I don't know why."

He accepted this. He was a farmer, used to the quirks of animals.

I gave him a treat to give Bella and then she was fine being close to him. We stayed another five minutes and then said goodbye.

When Kat and I debriefed out in the hallway, she asked me why I used treats. She added, "I can't use them with Wren; she is so food driven, she'll ignore the patients."

"Bella," I told her, "is the opposite. She only eats when she feels like it and doesn't steal the cat's food or take food off the table. But she often needs a treat as a lure, to help her over her shyness. Otherwise it's a struggle."

What just happened with the farmer was a perfect example.

As we walked toward another room, I added, "I don't know how else to get her close to the patients. If there were another way, I'd do it."

Rationally I knew that differences were okay, that all pet therapy teams were unique, and the work they did, the power they had to heal and comfort, were all the same. But part of me still felt like I was back in seventh grade, not fitting in. I wanted Kat to like me. I wanted her approval. And most of all, I wanted her to recognize that Bella was doing the best job she could.

She broke the tension by telling me that Wren once pulled a cast-iron pan off the stove, carried it in her teeth to the living room, not spilling a speck of food that was in the pan, and then devoured it.

"No!" I said, laughing.

"Oh, and a cup of coffee? She took the mug by the handle, then took it to where she could drink it without being found out."

Now I got it. This was a different creature—not a dog like Bella who grazed, ate a bit of her food, walked away, and finished it later if she felt like it.

We worked out an arrangement, visiting some rooms together, others separately. I noticed that Bella always did better with another dog, whether it was Wren, Boo, or Shelby. I think they kept her relaxed. I think she learned from them. It was like sharing gossip with a friend and I imagined they were telling each other: *Did you smell that guy?* or *Watch out for her. She's a grabber!*

As we rode the elevator down to the lobby, I watched Bella lick the side of Wren's mouth. I saw her shimmer with pleasure. For all her challenges, she was a wonderful dog. *And look*, I said to myself, *look how far she has come and what she can do.*

As we walked across the parking lot, I realized how individual this work was and how unique each team became. Bella's strengths and weaknesses were combined with my personality, who I was, and how I did things, to create a single impression, a single thing. A visit from Bella and me was unlike any other team. She and I brought our relationship, what we had learned about each other from hours of training and living together, to each encounter. And of course Kat and her dogs had their own style and chemistry, too.

In the past, I had jokingly referred to myself as Bella's chauffeur, the one who got her to work. But now I saw that that was inaccurate. It wasn't just her, it was us. It was who we were together.

And somehow the bond that we had together allowed others in. It invited them to closeness.

We gave the dogs time to stroll around on the patches of grass, and Kat put Wren back in her crate in the back of the van. Bella, proving that she did have an interest in food, poked her nose into a shopping bag on the floor in the back of her van and Kat laughed. The package inside was closed, but Bella knew they were dog treats.

On the way home, I asked her about her work as an evaluator of therapy dogs for Pet Partners, wondering, as she talked, if Bella would have passed her examination.

"The first thing I look for is that the dog and his or her handler are a team. They need to be confident and inspiring. As you know from doing this for a while, there are always distractions—always things that can make this hard for a dog. So I look to see how the team recovers from the unexpected."

I remembered Bella's test and how calm she was when they dropped pots and pans on the floor right next to her—surprising for a dog who cowers when it's windy. But I was by her side and didn't react, so maybe that helped.

"As I score a team, I pay attention to what the dog can do and what the handler does. And the handler must be so focused on the dog, so in tune, that the dog's safety comes first. This is work for them, but it's got to be safe work."

I nodded, hoping I didn't get so caught up in visiting patients that I forgot to watch for signs that Bella was tired or stressed out.

"And of course, the dog must be well groomed and healthy, and the handler has to engage well with people."

I thought about this for a moment and added, "And then there's sweetness."

"What?"

"I'm not saying this is part of the test, but your dogs and Bella are sweet. They have wonderful faces, great dispositions. They make people instantly like them."

Kat nodded and turned to smile at me. Our dogs were different, but we were on the same page.

Chapter 27

OUR VERY OWN SCHOOL

Fall 2013
Stonington, Connecticut

Bella, being part terrier, was sometimes identified as a pit bull, even though she didn't have that typical square head and jaw. Because pits have such a bad reputation, mostly unfairly, I corrected anyone who called her a pit bull and said that she was a blend of terrier, whippet, and lab. I often left out the Mexican Hairless breed that we thought she also had with her high body temperature and black skin, just because so few people knew that breed. Part of me was a lot like a pit bull—known for getting hold of things and not letting go. Back in the spring, while still working with Carol and Max at the Gales Ferry Elementary School, I launched a campaign to get Bella working at the elementary school five minutes from our home.

First I found out who the principal was and discovered that my brother-in-law, also an educator, knew him. So I wrote a friendly email, using this connection to introduce myself and

Bella. I mentioned what we'd done at the Gales Ferry School and suggested we meet. As the school year wasn't out yet, I knew the principal was busy, but I expected a response.

After a few weeks of hearing nothing back, I tried again. More nothing. Then I called and left a voicemail. Still no answer. Then I stopped by, without Bella, and told the school administrator who I was and that I was trying to reach the principal. He was out. A few more weeks went by, and now it was early summer 2013, and school was over for the year. I was confident he would get back to me, but he didn't. I loved the kids at Gales Ferry where we'd volunteered for the past six months, but realized it didn't make sense to spend more time driving than we did at the school. I wanted to be able to sustain this. Then I stopped by again, this time with Bella. The school administrator was not at all sure this was a good idea. I explained that she was a certified therapy dog and had worked successfully in another elementary school. I asked to see the principal. He was out again.

At my wit's end, I tried a new tactic: I wrote an email and put in the subject line: "Should I give up?" He called me the next day and we arranged to meet. I told myself to be careful not to share my frustration in reaching him. I got buzzed into the office and he came out to meet me. He was friendly and outgoing. We sat in his office and he told me a new special education teacher had been hired for the fall, and that she was very interested in having a therapy dog work with her students, but he wasn't sure it would work. They'd never had a dog at the school.

I told him it was amazing to see how dogs affected children. They shared a similar energy, they bonded instantly, and most important of all, the kids loved the dogs. They loved having this nonverbal affirmation. They loved the status of being the one with a dog at school. I asked if he'd like to talk with Carol or the school principal at the Gales Ferry School.

"I don't think that's necessary," he said. "What I think you should do is reach out to our new teacher and see what she wants."

I wanted to ask him if he was behind this program. But I didn't. Better to get the teacher on my side first, I thought.

He gave me her name and email and asked us to work it out. I left him copies of Bella's paperwork, certifications, and vet records, and told him I'd reach out to the new teacher, Aimée (pronounced *a-may*).

"We'd love to start in the fall," I told him before leaving the school.

As soon as I got home I told Bob (and Bella), "I think I did it! I've got to ask the teacher, but according to the principal, she's interested."

Bob knew me and wasn't surprised. *Persuasive* was the nice word. *Pushy* and *determined* might also be true.

The day after I emailed Aimée, she got back to me and said she had always wanted to see what a dog could do with her students. She was new to the school so she wanted to get her own routine settled before bringing Bella in, and she suggested we start the second week of school in September. I couldn't wait.

The summer went by quickly as it always did. Bella swam in the cove, all five grandkids visited—our daughter had three children ages seven, five and three, and our son had twin eight-month-old boys. They were adorable and we loved being part of their lives without the day-to-day responsibility. We lived out on our patio and threw tennis balls endlessly for Bella, who never tired of fetch. It was my favorite season; it slowed me down. I was happy to spend time outside in the garden and kayaking with Bob. We had always enjoyed our Connecticut summers, and we were loving being here year-round now.

My other projects continued: I taught my Boomer class, gave talks at libraries for people looking for work, and did publicity for my new book on interviewing that was coming out in the fall. I was finally over being let go from my job. This life—this flexible schedule with time for the work Bella and I did together, time to watch and simply notice things like the way the wind moves across the water—fit me so much better than my old schedule where I was always rushing not to fall behind. And then, suddenly it was Labor Day and time to check in with Aimée.

I got a strange note back from her. A cryptic "See the principal."

I told myself not to panic and sent him an email. He wrote back and said, "We have to talk." I made an appointment with his assistant and arrived at the school a few days later.

There was no small talk. He told me to sit down and said, "Don't think this is going to work."

"What? I worked this all out with Aimée and she's excited about having Bella here."

"There could be an allergy problem."

"A what?" My heart was racing and I tried not to scream.

"I met with the school nurse and she thinks it's a bad idea to have a dog in school. So many of our students have allergies."

I was stunned. Speechless.

"Thank you for trying," he added.

"Wait a minute. Bella goes into the hospital every week as well as a rehab facility. This doesn't make sense. If they let her in, if she gets in bed with cancer patients, she'll be fine in a school. And we won't go near children who have allergies. I keep her very clean and can wipe her down with an allergy wipe before we come to school."

"I don't know," he says. "The nurse—"

"The nurse shouldn't be making this decision. Of course the children must be kept safe, but Bella isn't going to make anyone sick. Do the special needs children have allergies? Do their parents not want them to see a dog in school?"

Now it was his turn to be stunned. He didn't have an answer.

"But she's against it," he repeated.

"Why would you lose the opportunity to have a therapy dog in your school? Can't we at least try it?"

I saw the tug of war going on in his head. The nurse had been there forever, but he wanted to make his new special ed teacher happy.

He took a deep breath. He saw that I wasn't giving up, that I believed this was an important chance to make a difference in these students' lives.

"Let's just do it," he said. "The nurse will get over it."

I exhaled. I got my breathing back under control. This was way too close. I felt like Jell-O inside.

We agreed on a date for Bella to start her visits, shook hands, and I left the school. In my car where no one could hear me, I said some terrible things about the nurse. A nurse I'd never met. A nurse who didn't know Bella. A nurse who almost stopped this program before it got started.

I wrote to Aimée and let her know we were still on. She asked me to come in after school to meet one of the students and his mother. She wrote that she thought it would help him to meet Bella with his family before working with her in school. I agreed and drove back to the school with Bella on a beautiful September day. As I pulled into the parking lot, I saw a mother with two children, and another woman who I assumed was Aimée.

The older child, a girl of about nine, started shouting the second Bella was out of the car: "Oh, look. A dog! A dog!" The boy, who turned out to be Liam, age six, got behind his mother.

I stopped about halfway to where they stood.

"Jean?" asked Aimée.

"Yes, I'm Jean and this is Bella."

The girl jumped off the sidewalk and ran toward Bella.

"I'm sorry but you're going to scare her. She's shy. Why don't you walk beside us?"

Aimée introduced me to Liam and his mother and told him that Bella and I would be coming to school every week to visit him. He looked more afraid than Bella. He looked as though this was a terrible idea.

"Would you like to help me hold the leash?" I asked him.

He shook his head.

Aimée suggested we go inside to the special ed classroom. I followed her, watching Liam to see if he was interested in Bella. His face was open and calm. Maybe on the edge of curious.

"This is our room," Liam told me. It was bright and cheerful with posters, books, thick mats on the floor, a swing on a tripod, and bright rubber balls of all sizes.

I liked the way he talked. His voice had a softness to it. Something sweet.

Bella saw the balls and looked interested. I slipped her a treat and told her she was a good girl. Liam kept his distance but was clearly intrigued that a dog was in school. Aimée explained to his mother that Liam would read to Bella and then they'd have a little play time.

"Has she done this before?" his mother asked me.

"Just last year, up in Gales Ferry. We worked with second graders and Bella was good with them."

"Liam is really afraid of dogs. I'm not sure how this will help him."

I turned to Aimée; she was the expert, not me.

"We'll go slowly and respect how close Liam wants to be to Bella. There are many studies that show dogs help children learn because they make them feel safe and relaxed. We're very excited to have Bella here."

Her ears perked up when she heard her name. If I could move mine, they'd be somewhere between up and back, flat against my head, as I was surprised by the questions. Surprised by the resistance.

I didn't volunteer that we'd never worked with children with special needs and that this was all new to us. By the time I got home, I was wondering why I worked so hard to get into this school. It wasn't like Gales Ferry, where we were added to an already existing program. We were the pioneers here, the first ones to bring pet therapy into the school. So of course it was going to be more difficult. But when I thought about Liam's face, his sandy brown hair, and the way he looked at Bella, the doubts faded and I was excited to find out what my dog could do.

When it was finally time for our first real visit, we met Aimée in the school office where I had to sign in and get a visitor sticker. The office was busy, and I liked seeing the double-take that the teachers and parents did when they saw a dog sitting by my side. Aimée told me that my first child would be Annelise, age six, legally blind. I was not prepared for a child who was still in diapers, who couldn't eat solid food, and who basically didn't talk. I sat down on the floor next to her and introduced myself. I met her paraprofessional educator, commonly called the para, named Kara, a wonderful young woman who seemed to have endless patience. Kara told me that Annelise loved music. I asked her if I could put a treat in her hand to give Bella. She couldn't answer so Kara opened her palm and I dropped a treat into it and Bella licked her hand.

"That was Bella," I said. Annelise stood and whirled in circles, around and around, her hands rubbing against each other. It made me dizzy to watch her.

We kept the visits short that first day, and after Annelise and Liam, we saw Austin. He had long, dark brown hair that flopped over his eyes, much of it matted. But he was clearly bright and loved to read. We sat down together on a pile of thick cushions.

"Can Bella sit with us?" I asked him.

He nodded but moved away so that she wasn't touching him. He then read us a book about pirates. He showed Bella the pictures.

"You're a great reader," I told him.

He nodded.

"Bella liked that book," I said, "although I think if she met a real pirate, she'd be afraid."

Austin jumped up off the cushions. "Don't be afraid, Bella. I'll get that pirate!"

I laughed and he threw himself back down on the cushions. Bella was startled but looked interested. Here was a strange creature indeed. Not at all like the sedate adults she lived with.

I gave Bella's tennis ball to Austin and suggested that he hide it. "Let's see how long it takes her to find it. Dogs have awesome noses and can smell where things are."

"Don't look, Bella," said Austin, turning his back on her and putting the ball on top of Aimée's desk.

"Ready?" I asked.

"Yup."

I let go of Bella's leash and she sniffed around the room, poking the cushions with her nose, trying to find the scent.

"She won't find it!" crowed Austin.

"Give her time. There are a lot of new smells for her in this room."

197

Just at that moment, Bella put her front paws up on the desk and very gently turned her head sideways to grab the ball with her mouth.

Austin clapped and I gave her a treat. "Well done, Bella," I added.

We talked for a few minutes and I told Austin that I would see him next week, then gathered my things and got ready to leave.

He gave me a high five and went into a separate room with his para to have his snack.

Aimée thanked me for coming and said that she was going to add a fourth child to our list in the next few weeks.

"That's fine," I said, knowing that she understood Bella couldn't do much more than an hour. As exciting as it was to finally be here, my first responsibility was always to make sure Bella was comfortable and safe.

Out in the hallway, I received startled looks from teachers and the kids were unable to stop themselves from saying, "Oh, look. A dog." Bella was pretty proud of herself and clearly loved the attention. This was not an easy assignment. Not at all. And for our first day, she did a really good job.

🐾 🐾

A few weeks later, as we learned how best to interact with these children, the local newspaper sent a reporter and a photographer to do a special article on Bella. Liam and I sat on the floor, and I tried get him a tiny bit closer to her. As the photographer snapped away, he reached out his hand, not touching her, but not shaking in fear either. A hello, a bridge. As this was going on, the reporter wanted to know Bella's story—where she came from, how she became a therapy dog, where else we worked. I used to think (like everyone else) that I was good at multitasking, but I realized then that I was terrible at it. I liked to do one thing at a time, so I felt tense trying to work with Liam and also answer her questions.

The reporter asked me to sit with Annelise so she could see how Bella did with her. Annelise whirled, Bella watched, and that was about it. But I tried—I always tried. And if Annelise laid down on her bean chair, which she often did, Bella was on her, licking her face, wagging her tail like crazy. She liked the smell of her diaper, too.

The paper could only photograph the two children whose parents signed releases, but the end result was wonderful— a front page article: "Dog with a 'great heart' is put to work at school." There were three photos—Bella with Liam, Bella with one of the huge yellow balls, a tennis ball in her mouth, and Bella with Annelise standing at her side. Aimée laminated the article and posted it in her room. The school had another copy put up in the entryway. Suddenly, Bella had gone from outsider to rock star status. So now, every time we walked down the hall, all we heard was "Hello, Bella," or "Hi, Bella," or "Look, it's Bella!" She couldn't tell me what this meant to her, but if I wasn't mistaken, she began to walk down the long school hallways with a bit of a swagger.

And for me, all the ups and downs, all the uncertainties of getting this project launched, evaporated. We were here where we wanted to be.

Chapter 28

SLOW IS THE NEW KINDNESS

Winter 2013–2014
Stonington, Connecticut

I have a vivid memory of a summer day on Cape Cod where I used to vacation. My daughter, Emily, was four years old and I was divorced—a single parent. I had met Bob and we had been dating for several months, but he was away, singing at a summer opera program. I left Emily off at her half-day summer camp and was turning my bike around to go home, a list of the ten things I hoped to accomplish swirling in my head, when I saw a man walking past a nearby house. He stopped, leaned down, and patted a fluffy black and white cat sunning himself in the driveway.

I was transfixed. He said something to the cat but I couldn't hear it. The cat rolled over on its back. The man scratched it behind the ears. What amazed me was that he stopped. He wasn't in a rush. He took time to visit with this cat. By being present, he was rewarded with this gift, this simple joy of greeting the cat.

I was thirty-three then and it took another thirty years before I could begin to let this lesson change me. It took losing my job, moving to Connecticut, trying and failing to replace the work I had been doing, and getting really tired. I called this driven energy being on a bulldozer. Scorch and burn—get things done no matter what the price.

Then one day, many years after seeing the cat, my tennis coach called me a "visionary" because I had the bad habit of looking where I thought the ball would go, rather than at the ball itself. It was a really bad way to play tennis. So now, I mostly looked at the ball. I subtracted "must-do's" from my day, I gave myself quiet time, I wrote in my journal, took long walks, got seaweed off the beach for my garden. And yes, I worked, too. I was still a type A or AAA, as Bob says. But I tempered my pace. I said no to commitments that weren't what I wanted to do. Mostly I learned from Bella, who, like me, was so fast she was a white blur, that I wouldn't die if I slowed down. I would be okay if I stopped. I didn't have to prove anything. No matter what she was doing, she was present, and time stood still. She was really good at changing gears, too. She could flop down on the floor and be fast asleep a minute after chasing Henry around the house.

I finally figured out that this was where kindness was born. You really couldn't be kind if you were in a hurry, if you were thinking about the next thing. Slow was the new kindness. It was a discipline. A way of being. And linked to that, similar in many ways, was what I was learning from the people Bella and I visited, especially the rehab residents. As Anne LaMotte said in her wonderful book on life and writing, *Bird by Bird*, "Dying people teach you to pay attention and forgive and not to sweat the small things." Dying people and dogs.

In the crazy season between Thanksgiving and Christmas, I caught a cold and had to cancel my work with Bella. At first it was nice staying in bed, Bella and Henry curled up next to me. And Bob took good care of me, making me healthy lunches and bringing me endless cups of tea. But after two days of this, I was bored. I needed to do something but didn't have the energy and couldn't risk getting other people sick. Without getting things done, without interacting with other people (yes, I was a classic extrovert), my life felt flat. Bella adjusted to this new schedule without any problem and took advantage of being able to get away with things she couldn't ordinarily do, like pull the stuffing out of all her toys. I laid in bed and watched her rip each toy open and then extract the stuffing. One piece stuck to the side of her jaw and made me laugh: "Look at you, Bella. You're foaming at the mouth." She was in heaven, destruction being one of the highest forms of joy. The rug looked like a cotton field. I was careful to make sure she didn't eat the squeakers.

When there was nothing else to rip apart, she came back to bed and fell fast asleep. She must have been dreaming of running as her feet twitched and she made little yipping sounds. Henry was on the other side of me purring. It was a symphony, and I took a little nap sandwiched between my two buddies.

As soon as I felt better, I got back to my regular schedule, happy to be working with Bella and teaching my class on top of getting ready for Christmas. I told myself to remember slowness, to not let my energy drive me past noticing. I took mini-breaks. I looked out the window at the cove, watched the ice coating the rocks along the shore, and understood that the stillness that came out of the whirlwind was the most profound, and the most difficult, to achieve.

Along with slowness, I learned about devotion. About the kind of love that showed up no matter how difficult it was. The spouses and sometimes the grown children of the rehab residents were teaching me this. They were here week after week. They brought in holiday decorations and took them out again. They brought in food and hand-knitted shawls. Sometimes photo albums. Special blankets. Treats.

Nancy did her mother's nails. She made sure she was well dressed. She brought in a radio so Alice could listen to music. She got her hair done. And one day when I told her what a wonderful daughter she was, she made a face.

"What?" I asked.

"I do what I can."

"Which is a whole lot," I told her.

She didn't tell me the details but shared that her mother was "difficult." Not an easy person to have as a Mom. In many ways, Nancy had to raise herself.

"But how can you do so much for her if she was like that?" I asked.

"It doesn't matter," said Nancy. "She's my mother. I took care of my father, too, before he died."

Now I thought she was a saint. Did she have any time for herself?

"Wow," I said.

"You get into it—you learn. But the bad days are hard."

And I thought, *Yes, when you make an effort and it's misunderstood or not appreciated, that's a huge test. That pushes you to the wall.*

As if reading my mind, she said, "The dogs are a big help. They really are. I always look forward to Wednesdays."

Deb and I hugged Nancy, I blew a kiss to Alice who blew one back, and we said good-bye and went back out into the hall.

"My parents died suddenly," I told Deb, "so I have no experience in this. Have no way to know how to do it day in and day out."

I'd seen other people doing it. When my father-in-law, who had Alzheimer's, had to be institutionalized, Bob's mother went several times a week to visit him: she held his hand, brought him food, did whatever she could to comfort him. And when my own son was hospitalized at age two with Lyme disease, I met a woman whose infant son was dying of a serious heart condition. She was there around the clock, holding him, singing to him, making his short life as whole as she could. The baby's name was Henrico.

I had the feeling that this is where real love is born. Not in the easy stuff, not in the romance found in movies and books, but here, where life was stripped down to its essentials. Where it was hard to show up week after week, where it felt as if love was a one-way street, as these families at the rehab facility knew all too well.

🐾 🐾

There were a few couples who shared a room—together in this last phase. Last place. One couple interacted actively with each other, while another seemed like two ships in separate oceans. The husband of this couple, Jeff, was a riot. He loved the dogs and made little squealing sounds when we walked through the door. Mostly his wife, on the other side of the room, ignored us. One of their kids or grandkids had made a huge collage of photos of them posted on the wall. I looked at them—getting married, holding babies, having family cook-outs, and it didn't seem possible that these people, these two old people in this room, were related to those vibrant images.

Jeff said things like, "Oh, look at you!" and loved to run his hand up and down the dogs' backs, ruffling their fur. Shelby stood still, enjoying the attention. Bella backed up but then put her paws up on his lap if I lured her with a treat. He giggled. He made sounds that were more dog than English. His face was young and happy for those brief moments. Deb did a wicked imitation of him that cracked me up, but she never did it in his room. One day, while Jeff was having his love fest with the dogs, we heard his wife say in a clear voice, "She's backing away."

I turned to look at her and saw that she was watching Bella with her husband.

"Yes," I told her. "You're right. She's shy."

"She backed away," she repeated.

"Doesn't like to be touched on the head," I added.

"Look at that," she said with real interest. "Nice dogs."

Deb added, "Yes, they are."

"See you next week," I told both of them. "Take care."

She nodded and smiled, Jeff waved.

Out in the hall, Deb looked at me. "Wow, that was a surprise."

"And we thought she didn't respond to the dogs."

It was impossible not to make judgments, not to focus on the ones who gave us the most feedback. We tried hard to include everyone, but some turned us away, others were too trapped by pain or by what was happening to them to react, and as we'd just learned from Jeff's wife, sometimes our impressions were wrong.

We followed our dogs down the hallway, in awe of the doors they opened. Endlessly surprised by the things they could do.

Other couples didn't live together but still spent a lot of time with each other. Our favorite was Mary. She had pale white skin, gray hair, and a loud voice because she was hard of hearing. Her husband, Alphonse, was almost always visiting, sitting on a chair beside her bed and holding her hand. I loved this. It was sort of like they were teenagers only they were both in their eighties or nineties.

On one visit when there was music on the TV, I said to Alphonse, "Doesn't this make you want to dance?"

And a huge smile burst across his face and he told me, "Mary was a great dancer. She loved it. We'd go out every chance we got and dance until we couldn't stand up."

I looked at her, barely able to sit up in her bed, and imagined her in a brightly colored dress, stockings, heels, swing dancing the night away. I hoped she had those memories. I hoped her heart was still dancing.

Bella put her feet up on the edge of Mary's bed. Mary's eyebrows shot up and she said, "Oh, look!" And Alphonse grinned and said that the dogs were here.

"She's so . . . and the other one is, too."

She looked from Bella to Shelby.

"Yes," I told her. "They came to visit you."

Bella hopped down when treats were no longer being offered. Mary followed her with her eyes while her roommate, Barbara, smiled and nodded. Her wall was covered with pictures of horses and her bedspread had a collage of colts running in a field. She wore dark glasses so we never saw her eyes. Her TV was blaring, as was Mary's, but behind all the chatter was quiet. It was a safe place to be. The pale winter sun slanted in the window, the colts raced, and Mary was hand-in-hand with her husband of fifty-eight years. No one was in a hurry.

Months later, a new patient moved into the room right before the dining room. Deb and I hesitated, as there was no name posted outside the room. We could see it was a man, but not much else. He looked like a mummy tightly wrapped in blankets.

Deb looked at me with her eyebrows up and I nodded. We'd give it a try. We approached the bed slowly, and I asked in a soft voice, "Would you like to see the dogs?"

A bruised and swollen face emerged from the blankets and we saw a slight nod. Deb told him the names of the dogs and his eyes followed them. We didn't dare get the dogs too close, as he'd obviously fallen or somehow had a bad injury. His mouth opened and he said, "Mary.'"

I jumped back as if hit by an electric current. It was Alphonse. Deb didn't believe it, but I knew it was him.

"Oh, my God, Alphonse. What happened to you?"

"Fell," he said simply, conserving his energy.

"We just saw Mary and she's fine, but of course she misses you." He shook his head.

Deb added, "We'll tell her we saw you."

He nodded.

We promised we'd visit every week, and we did until about a month later, when we were told that he had died. He didn't make it.

"What will Mary do?" I asked Deb.

"I don't know."

We were afraid to go into her room, but made ourselves do it. She wasn't interested in the dogs, but told Deb and me, "My husband died."

I took her hand and told her how sorry I was. Deb reminded her that we visited Alphonse every week and told her what a wonderful husband he was.

"He'll be here tomorrow," she said in a strong voice. A certain voice.

"Oh?" I said, not sure where this was going.

"He had errands today, but I'll see him tomorrow."

And as we left the room, I said quietly to myself, "Yes, you will. You certainly will."

Chapter 29

LEGACY FROM ANGUS

Winter 2014
Stonington, Connecticut

It was a winter of snow, swirling winds, and cold. But I loved it. My son gave me snow pants for Christmas so I could bundle up like a little kid and stay warm. When Deb and I had started going to The Starfish Home with the dogs a year and a half earlier, she was also going to a hospital in Rhode Island. But then she decided it would be more fun to go to the hospital in New London where Bella and I went. Once she got her paperwork in order, we met at the volunteer office, Deb in her brand new blue jacket. I watched Bella and Shelby walk close to each other while Deb and I caught up. We were a pack—a unit that was more than the sum of its parts.

As we headed down one of the echoing hallways, we heard a voice. A clear, loud voice that said, "I see dogs. Dogs are in the hospital."

We looked around, but the hallway was empty. We kept walking and the voice said, "I'm so glad dogs are here today."

Now Deb and I were smiling, although we still didn't know who was talking. As we rounded a corner, we saw a man about our age waiting for us.

"Well, here you are. I was pretty sure I heard their tags jangling and figured it had to be dogs!"

Deb and I nodded while he gave them a pat.

"Therapy dogs?" he asked, while Shelby leaned up against his legs.

"Yes," said Deb.

"Bless you," he said. "Oh dear," he added. "My manners. I'm a chaplain, a Jewish chaplain, and I can't tell you what these animals do. How wonderful they are."

"We know," I added, grinning at him, thinking that his job was so much harder, as he had to do it alone.

Deb said, "When we heard your voice it was like the Wizard of Oz!"

He laughed and told us to keep up the good work. And then he was off, while Deb and I looked at each other and shook our heads.

L&M hospital had built a new facility for cancer patients nearby. It was beautiful with Zen gardens outside, large glass windows, plants and flowers everywhere, even a basket with hand-knitted hats, free for any of the patients. To volunteer there we had to wear beige jackets and had to have an additional blood test to make sure we wouldn't endanger any of the patients. Radiation was on the ground floor. The waiting room and the chemo suites where we could visit were on the second floor.

On our first time there, a nurse asked us to go into a private room where a blind patient was receiving chemo. I knocked on the door and when she said "Come in," we walked over to her bed and I told her that Deb and I and our two dogs were here to visit.

"Oh, I love dogs."

I noticed she had an accent and asked her where she was from. "Puerto Rico."

"Just like Bella," I told her, and gave her the bland version of Bella's story, leaving out the Dead Dog Beach part.

She and I chatted in Spanish for a bit, my vocabulary making this a simple exchange. As we talked, I watched her face and it was amazing, like reading a book, I could see moods and colors crossing her face. We learned she used to have a dog but that it had died. She told us about how she learned to cook without being able to see. And she had an assistant who came in a few times a week to help her with the things she couldn't do.

What I loved about this woman was that she didn't feel sorry for herself. She seemed at peace with blindness, cancer, whatever was thrown at her. Shelby got close enough to her bed that she could pet her, and Bella had a turn, too, with her front paws up on the side of her bed. As we said good-bye, I felt as though I was leaving a party, a wonderful, short party where people connected and cared about each other.

In reading studies about how therapy dogs worked, it was interesting that long visits weren't necessary. Short was fine as long as the teams were attentive and caring. I wondered what picture this woman had of the two dogs. How—from the texture of their fur and the way they moved and smelled, the sound of their nails on the floor—she created an image of the whole dog.

Deb could only join us once in a while, and as Bella and I visited by ourselves more often, I began to notice something about the cancer patients: they seemed to fall into categories. There were the fighters who were going to beat this thing no matter what it took. Even in pain, they seemed optimistic. They looked forward.

They could imagine themselves not ill. Then there were ones who accepted this illness in a spiritual way—as part of life, part of a mystery. They didn't ask why, didn't complain, just quietly worked through it. They were polite to the staff and thanked us for visiting. And as one woman said to me, "I'm covered in prayer," and it was so real, I felt I could see it.

Then there were those who were afraid, whose fear was palpable. Present. The dogs were a quick distraction, but didn't touch it, didn't take it away. They'd been invaded, their bodies were attacking themselves. They were going to die. Still, others found a kind of dark humor—they made jokes about the chemo, about glowing in the dark from radiation, and their laughter freed them, even if only for a moment. And some were angry. Really ticked off.

I got a request from the volunteer coordinator to visit a man named Joe at the Cancer Center. He was there every Tuesday morning and had asked for a dog to visit. In the lobby, I signed in, walked upstairs with Bella, visited with a few patients who were in the large waiting area with their families, and then found Joe. He looked to me to be in his mid to late sixties. Just like me.

"Hi," I said. "I'm Jean and this is Bella. I heard you wanted a visit from a dog."

His face was expressionless. He didn't react to Bella. His wife sat off to the side.

"What kind of dog is she?" he asked.

"A mix. Mostly lab, but whippet, terrier too. She's a rescue."

He wasn't interested in her story.

"Would you like to give her a treat?"

A slight nod. I put one in his hand and Bella put her front paws up on the edge of his recliner and took the treat from his hand. We chatted for a few minutes and I asked him if he'd like us to come back.

"Okay," he said with no enthusiasm.

After a few weeks of weekly visits, Joe said to me, "This is poison."

I hesitated, not sure what to say.

"I'm here getting poisoned, so if the cancer doesn't kill me, the drugs will."

I looked at the clear tube connected to the port in his chest. His wife had her head buried in a book.

"But isn't this supposed to give you a chance?" I asked, breaking the rules about asking patients about their health.

He busted out laughing, a harsh sound with no joy in it. "That's what they say. You can believe what you want."

I didn't know what to believe, but had the feeling that if he thought this would kill him, it probably would. We saw him for a few more weeks and then his schedule changed and he didn't ask for any more visits from a dog.

Other patients were at a crossroads, their lives divided into two distinct sections: before cancer and after cancer. They changed. They lost parts of themselves but became more outspoken. This seemed to be what had happened to my best friend from college, Nancy.

The nightmare had come true. Her mother died of melanoma in her early fifties, and Nancy, in her late sixties, received the diagnosis that she had breast cancer. She didn't tell me until she had started chemo.

"Oh, my God," I said, stunned, saddened, afraid for her.

"I'm going to beat it," she told me.

The doctors gave her an 88 percent chance of survival. I knew that was hopeful, but I couldn't help thinking about the 12 percent. The what ifs.

We talked on the phone and I found out that her life now revolved around her treatments. There were endless doctor visits, trips to New York City, studies, specialists, hours and hours of chemo. It was exhausting. No, it was worse than that. It was counter-intuitive. Chemo was an invasion, poison, something harmful that was one of the few weapons in this war. And it was cumulative. So week one, Nancy thought it wasn't so bad, but by week three or four, she'd gotten sores in her mouth, couldn't sleep because of night panics, a port in her chest that never stopped hurting, and later on, when she was further into her treatment, her husband had to give her shots in the stomach twice a day because of a blood clot. And then the steroids, which were necessary to reduce inflammation, put her on an emotional roller coaster. She cried at the drop of a hat.

But she didn't tell me this then. She kept it to herself, just the way my cousin Linda did. And when I asked Nancy why, why she couldn't tell me then what she was going through, she said simply, "The sick live in a different world. A world so separate, so cut off, that there are no phone lines, no communication between them."

I was stunned, but believed she was right. Back when Nancy started her treatment, I asked a neighbor, who had survived brain cancer, for advice. I wanted her ideas about how I could best support Nancy through this ordeal.

"Someone gave me a shoe box with gifts in it—little things like hand lotion, a pen, chapstick. And there were notes in it too. Inspirational sayings. So when I had a really bad day, when the pain got to me, I'd pull out the box and open something."

"Oh," I had replied. "I love that."

That gave me a task. I had kept a clear, Lucite paint bucket that Nancy had given me my birthday gift in a few years back, and for several weeks, I filled it with treats. I found a website that sold headgear for cancer patients and bought a soft red head-covering for when her hair fell out. I added notes, being careful not to sound too upbeat, as I suspected that could be really annoying. When it was full, I wrote "Nancy's recovery bucket" on it and mailed it to her. She loved it. I suspected she opened most of the gifts at once, but I didn't ask, as it was hers and she could do whatever she wanted with it.

She endured, didn't complain, and was finally in remission. I thought this was good, the worst was over, and we could get on with things. In one of our phone calls, I asked Nancy if she and her husband, Bill, would like to visit us. There was a long pause.

"Something wrong?" I asked.

"Yes, in fact there is. I can't do things on your terms anymore."

Now I was stunned. What was she talking about?

"What?"

"You want things your way. You expect me to go along, but I can't. I'm not that person anymore."

I felt heat traveling to my face and a knee-jerk reaction to hit back. To hurt because I'd been hurt.

"I don't get that," I had said as quietly as I could.

"That's right. You don't."

"I've got to go. We'll talk again soon." And I had hung up the phone.

Weeks went by and I replayed this conversation over and over. What was her problem? Why was she striking out at me, her oldest and best friend?

I sent her a card. We chatted a few times. But we were cautious strangers, not friends. Not friends of forty years. Not the friends who met in college and moved to New York City about the same time.

But somehow, we kept the door open a crack. The ice started to melt. Friendship and our long history won out. And I figured out that I needed to make the effort to understand who she was now. I offered to visit her. She lived on Long Island, so on a beautiful June summer day, I took the ferry from New London to Orient Point. I was nervous. This was either going to be a really good way for us to reconnect, or it was going to be awful.

By mistake, she went to a different ferry terminal and it took almost two hours before she arrived to pick me up. But I didn't mind. I sat by the water, bought a cup of tea from a concession stand, and waited. Without realizing it, I put myself into that slow and open place that I had discovered from my work with Bella. We had a good weekend together, and she told me about what she went through, about the pain and the fear, and about how she calculated life differently now; it was more like standing on something that could give way at any moment instead of solid ground. I saw the courage it took to live this way, and we became better friends than ever.

🐾 🐾

It was another cold winter day, early in 2014, and as I vacuumed the deep red rug in my dining room, I thought about the friend back in Pennsylvania who gave it to me. (Actually, her daughters gave it to me after she died ten years ago.) Ann and I went to the same church, both sang in a funky little choir, and when she was diagnosed with stage-four stomach cancer, I became part of her support team. This was before Bella's time, when we still had Angus. I brought her food when she could still eat, drove her to hospital visits, and stopped by to keep her company. Her daughters were wonderful and I enjoyed getting to know them, too.

But then everything fell apart. The pain was too much. The feeding tube was problematic, and despite blood infusions, she was dying. Ann was one of the most stubborn people I've ever known. She worked way longer than was humanly possible, overcoming crippling pain and never complaining. But the day came when she couldn't work, and finally her daughters told her, after she had been hospitalized for several days, that she couldn't go home again.

They told her it was time for hospice. She had a choice—hospice or a nursing home.

She screamed with the tiny bit of energy she had left, she told them she wanted to go home, she said it was unfair, but they insisted she wasn't safe at home any longer, that her cancer was advancing and she needed more care. She picked hospice. It turned out to be a wonderful place. There were hand-made quilts on the walls, soft pillows, bird feeders outside the windows, music, massages, a kitchen with homemade cookies for the visitors, and a culture of caring.

Somehow I got the idea that I would bring Angus there, maybe more to comfort myself instead of Ann, as I was nervous about going to a hospice facility. This was brand new for me—uncharted territory. Ann's daughters thought it was a good idea, and when I called the facility, they said it was fine as long as I had proof that my dog's rabies vaccination was up to date. Angus, at this point about fourteen years old, needed a little help getting in and out of the car, but walked into this facility as if he had been doing this his whole life.

We signed in at the front desk, I gave them a copy of his veterinary records, and asked for directions to the hospice wing. We found Ann's room, and her daughters and one of their husbands were there. Ann looked like a twig smothered by blankets. I knelt down beside her bed so that I was at her eye level and Angus came up beside me.

"We came to see you," I told her. "Angus came, too."

One hand reached out and touched his thick fur. He leaned into her hand. Everyone in the room waited. It was as if time itself held its breath.

She didn't have the strength to do anything else. She couldn't talk. I gently stroked her arm and talked to her. I knew not to stay too long, but before I left, I had to tell her something.

"I love you, Ann," I had said, bending close to her ear. "You fought hard, you did a good job, but it's time to let go. You don't have to struggle anymore."

Her face relaxed.

"And there are angels who will fold you in their wings. I know there are."

Tears were streaming down my face and I couldn't even say good-bye. The daughters thanked me and I left the room. As I walked past the dining room, which was full of the nursing home patients, an aide asked me if I'd mind going in with my dog. I wiped the tears off my face and followed her in. Some patients didn't react, but one man, slumped in his wheelchair, put out his hand and said, "Collie."

"Yes," I responded. "Yes, Angus is a collie."

Angus worked the room, wagging his plume-like tail, gentle, kind, unafraid of this new place. I followed, amazed and yet not totally surprised. This was so in character for him.

Once outside, I let Angus walk slowly through the grass, and carefully put him back in the car. "You did a good job, Angus," I told him, not knowing that at that exact moment, a few hours before Ann died, my new vocation was born.

Two years later, on a beautiful June day, we had Angus put down. Here was the poem I wrote in his memory a few months later. All of it true:

> When you ate
> The lights off the Christmas tree,
> We returned.
> When you made it clear

The kennel was not for you,
We got you out.
When you told us
You were meant to be
With us always,
We acquiesced.
When you said we talked
Too much and needed
To be on the floor,
You drew us to your level.
But best perhaps
Was the welcome:
Joy breaking out
At just the sight of us,
Tail shimmering, full body
Jubilation as if
At that moment
We had been recreated
Out of thin air.

So how do you say goodbye
To that kind of love?
How fill the emptiness?
You can't, you say,
But still, hanging in the air,
Like mist after rain
Is the promise
That you are waiting,
And will welcome us again.

September 2006

Chapter 30

AT THE END THERE IS A DOG

Winter and Spring 2014
Stonington, Connecticut

It was hard to remember that when Bella first met Shelby, she didn't like her—hackles raised, she had let out a low growl. But now all I had to say was "Bella, we're going to see Shelby," and she raced for the back door, tail wagging. Deb and I were the same way. We'd become sisters, trusting each other, laughing at ourselves and at the situations we got ourselves in. If we had tails, we'd wag them like crazy at just the sight of each other. It was good we had this bond, because some days everything was a bit off.

One day, as we walked in the front door of the rehab facility, Bella saw Nancy in the lounge helping the residents play Bingo and threw her head back, letting out a loud howl. It was like electricity, all eyes on her. Nancy radiated surprise and then pleasure that this exuberant welcome was for her.

"No, Bella. Quiet!" I had commanded, shocked that my well-trained therapy dog would cause such a scene.

"It's okay," Nancy had said while Deb looked at Bella and laughed. "She's a character, isn't she?" she added.

I apologized to the group and we began our visits. Shelby dragged Deb into Abby's room, but Abby had been moved because of an infection. Shelby looked around, not sure where the lady had gone with her salmon and bacon treats. Bella stood close behind Shelby, waiting to see what would happen.

"She's not here," Deb told the dogs. "Come on."

We left Abby's former room, talking about how much she loved the dogs, how even in her empty room we could see her bending over the treats and selecting the very best for her two hungry friends.

"I can't go by her new room," Deb said. "She'll have a fit if she sees Shelby and can't pet her."

"We could wave," I suggested, knowing we weren't allowed to visit her while her infection was contagious.

Deb looked at me and made a face. When we got to her new room, Bella and I raced past her door, hoping she didn't see us, while Deb and Shelby made a huge detour.

Michael had been moved, too, and was pissed off. He wanted his old room back and didn't care that it was being renovated. He pointed to the extra bed in his new room and told us, "I'd like to get a girl in there."

Deb and I stood still, speechless.

"See that pink bucket?" he added.

There was a pink plastic wash basin on this bed.

"Right by that bucket, I'd like to—"

"Hey, Michael," I interrupted. "Can Bella say hello?"

He looked at her, distracted, disappointed, clearly letting us know that we were as annoying as the staff. He was so young and so ruined. Betrayed by his body.

"I need to see Bonnie," he said.

Deb had stepped out into the hallway with Shelby.

"I'm happy to give her a message."

"Yeah, I need to talk to her. I can't stand this room."

"Okay, I'll tell her. See you next week?"

He turned his head away from me and looked out the window. Bella pulled me toward the door, anxious to be back with Shelby. I wasn't good at admitting defeat, but right then, right there, I knew that visits from two wonderful dogs weren't making much of a difference. Not in his world.

🐾 🐾

The school was another matter. We were now nearing the end of the school year and had a workable routine. After signing in at the front desk and getting a visitor pass, we went down the long hallway to the special education classroom. Bella and I spent about fifteen to twenty minutes with each child, starting with reading time, then played with the tennis ball, walked down the hallway, or on nice days, went outside.

Annelise had warmed up to us a bit and sometimes flung herself in my lap. The para told me to be careful—she bit. We sang songs together and sometimes danced. Bella looked on with her head cocked to one side as if asking, "What on earth are you doing? Do I know you?"

As we were chatting, Aimée came up, and after listening for a while, said, "Oh, it's you."

"It's me what?" I asked.

"You're the one who says *girlfriend.*"

I nodded, as it was one of several nicknames I called Bella.

"Why?" I asked.

"Annelise lives with her grandparents, and as you know, doesn't talk much. But over the weekend she apparently kept saying *girl-friend.* Now we know where she got it."

I laughed, thinking to myself it was a good thing I didn't say something worse.

Liam and I sat together on huge pillows on the floor. He had two obsessions: pirates and dinosaurs. He selected a book on one of these two topics and then "read" it to me and Bella. He couldn't read, but he looked carefully at the pictures and then explained the story to me. Here's how he read the dinosaur book to me:

> *Page 1—Bones*
> *Page 2—Eggs*
> *Page 3—Sharp teeth*
> *Page 4—Dead*
> *Page 5—Bones, eggs*
> *Page 6—Extinct*
> *Page 7—Dead*
> *Page 8—Bones*
> *Page 9—Teeth*
> *Page 10—Dead*
> *Page 11—And they all lived happily ever after*

"Wow," I said, "good reading. Bella liked it, too." Bella was curled up near his feet, but didn't touch him. He was still afraid, although his para told me that he talked about Bella all week, saying over and over, "I want to see Bella." And on good days, when he was feeling brave, he touched her back and I watched his face, the face of a boy discovering a miracle.

There was something wonderful about being on these pillows with this boy. This boy and my dog. I always told him he did a good job, and that I couldn't wait to see him the next week. He was growing so fast that his pants barely made it to his ankles. I couldn't imagine his future, didn't know if he'd ever master reading, but I hoped that somewhere in his memory there would be a white dog who loved to listen to him.

Next we saw Austin. He was a firecracker, all energy, his wild hair flopped over his face. He found Bella funny and gave her math problems to solve.

"Okay, Bella," he said, pulling out a container of blocks. "How much is ten minus four?"

Bella looked puzzled, and then said, "Five?" (Well I said "five" out of the corner of my mouth.)

"No, Bella. Wrong!" shouted Austin. "Try again."

"Let me see, six?"

"Yes, yes—you got it right!" Austin jumped up in the air and then did a somersault.

"Let's do Olympics," he said, the blocks quickly forgotten.

"Okay," I said, now speaking for myself, not Bella. "Just put away the blocks so you don't trip over them."

He backed up, made a running leap, and did two somersaults on the thick floor mats.

"Now your turn."

"I'm not sure I can do that, Austin."

"You can—yes you can!"

I got down on my hands and knees, wondering how many years it had been since I did a somersault.

"Go!" shouted Austin. "It's the Olympics." His para watched in disbelief as I got my sixty-seven-year-old body to flip over.

"Oh, that was terrible," I told him as the room spun.

"Again!"

"No thanks, Austin. It's your turn."

And then, his creativity on speed, he made up names for all the stunts he did and Bella and I watched. When our time was over he said, "Good-bye, Jean. Good-bye, Bella," his eyes sparkling with excitement. And just as he reached the door, he turned back and added, "Bella is precious." That was one of my mother's favorite words, and I felt what could become a sob catch in my throat.

There were two other boys we saw that first year in the school, but because we were not on a regular schedule, we didn't grow as close. But one boy drew a picture of Bella for me, and when we read, I noticed he always leaned up against my shoulder.

When school was almost over, Aimée asked me if Bella would go with Austin to the auditorium, as he hated to have his photo taken and it was school picture day. We stood in line together, the other children looking at Bella, wanting to pet her.

"Sorry," I told them. "She's working right now. This is her time with Austin."

When it was our turn, we walked up the stairs to the stage where the photographer was set up. Austin stayed with us until he saw the camera. Then he jumped off the stage.

"Come back," I told him. "Look—Bella's not afraid."

He laughed and ran off so Bella got her portrait done without him. She didn't seem to mind the bright lights. Lynn, his wonderful para, thanked me for trying. I was in awe of her and the others— of their patience, their love for these children, and the endless ways they were present. I thought to myself that they should be earning the big bucks instead of athletes or rock stars. Their jobs were a whole lot harder. And more important.

🐾 🐾

Deb and I went up to the fifth floor of the hospital, careful to avoid one wing where there was a nurse terrified of dogs. Deb had followed me on our first few visits here together, but now she was just as comfortable as she was at Starfish.

We walked into one room and the man in the near bed was asleep, so we spent time with his roommate. He liked dogs and wanted to know their stories. We said good-bye and were almost out of the room when the other man woke up and said in a loud voice, "Oh my God! Dogs!"

Deb and I froze, not sure if this was an invitation or a signal to get out of the room quickly.

"Would you like to see them?" I asked, holding my breath.

"Yes. Oh, yes! I love dogs."

I got Bella to put her paws up on the edge of his bed and he fed her a treat.

"Oh, look at her. She's beautiful."

I saw tears sliding down the side of his face.

"Let me see the other one."

Deb brought Shelby over and he reached his hand down to pet her silky fur. Shelby looked very pleased with herself.

"I miss my dog," he said quietly.

As we talked, we found out that his dog, a lab mix, had died eight years ago, but right now in this room, it was yesterday—the loss, his dog's boundless love, and all the things they did together.

"It's hard, isn't it?" I asked, thinking of Angus.

He nodded, and Deb and I were quiet while he pet Bella and Shelby. Just as we were about to say good-bye, he stopped us.

"I don't have much time."

"You're getting out soon?" asked Deb.

"No. Not much more time."

And when we still didn't get it, he added, "I'm dying."

"Oh," I said, "I'm sorry."

He didn't want to talk about this, and the tears that had been sliding from the corners of his eyes were now streaming down his cheeks.

"But you brought in dogs. You gave me something. I will never forget you."

Deb and I fought back our own tears while Bella and Shelby looked up at us wondering what to do next. We stayed, we talked to him, we were there as long as he wanted us to be. But when his face looked tired, we gently said good-bye. And as he closed his eyes, we saw a slight smile and a look of peace on his face.

Out in the hallway, Deb said, "Oh, my God."

"I know."

"I've never—"

"I know."

We decided to visit a few more rooms before leaving. A nurse asked us to see a patient on the other side of the ward. He was a young man, probably in his twenties, lying in bed with a nurse sitting in a chair near the foot of the bed monitoring him. We didn't know why and couldn't ask.

For the second time that day, we received an exuberant reception. He was not content to lie still with two dogs in his room, and asked the nurse to help him sit up. She did and he swung his legs over the edge of the bed so he could get closer to Bella and Shelby. Bella took this as an invitation to jump up on his bed next to him.

"Oh," he said, "you're a cutie. Yes, you are."

He put his arm around Bella and I stopped myself from telling him that Bella was head-shy, as she clearly wasn't anything shy. She licked the side of his face while Shelby pressed herself up against his legs.

"This is fantastic!" he said. "You brought me fur angels. Two beautiful fur angels."

Deb and I were on the verge of tears for the second time that day and couldn't look at each other. But like proud parents, we watched our dogs, astonished by what they did.

A few weeks later, as Bella and I were visiting the residents at Starfish, (Deb had a conflict and couldn't be there), and we were just passing the nurses' station, just a few rooms from Beverly's, I heard someone calling my name.

An aide rushed up the hallway. "Wait, Jean. Wait a minute."

I hesitated, wondering what was up. Bella had her head cocked to one side.

"Need to talk with you."

"Okay," I said, waiting.

"I didn't want you to find out in her room. I wanted to tell you that Beverly died over the weekend."

"What?" I felt as if someone had punched me in the stomach.

"She was doing okay but then her head dropped down onto her chest, so the aide put her in bed. The nurse checked on her, but after some time, she stopped breathing and quietly slipped away."

All I could envision was the way her closed-in face, a face sometimes as dark as a thunderstorm, broke open into a wild grin with half her teeth missing and the others black, and the way her eyes always held pure mischief. She and I shared so many jokes—jokes with no words, just two girls laughing. Girls in their sixties and eighties, that is.

I tried to get my breathing back to normal. I tried to take in what she was telling me. I had known it would happen at some point, but I wasn't ready. I stood in the hallway and couldn't move.

"I'm so sorry, Jean," added the aide.

I thanked her for telling me. I don't remember what I did next, but somehow I got back out to my car, Bella curled up in the back seat, the windows open.

"No," I whispered to the soft spring air. "Not Beverly."

I could see her face, I could feel her hand on my wrist, and I suddenly realized that the dolls Beverly always held (her "babies" as I called them), were me. In some inexplicable way, Beverly had become my mother. She had patted my hand, straightened the sleeve of my sweater, and held me in her gaze as she rocked her babies. I took to calling her My Beverly. And Deb often told me, "She loves you."

But now her bed was empty, the dolls abandoned, and I couldn't get my mind to accept she was gone. How could it be that an Alzheimer's patient with brittle diabetes, in only two years of weekly visits, had become my surrogate mother?

I always said to her, "See you next week, Beverly." But now I wouldn't. And while I cared about the other residents, no one would hold me the way she did. No one would crack my heart open with a grin from the dark place where she was trapped.

A few more weeks went by and I still had a hard time going to Starfish. I cared about the other residents, but Beverly's absence weighed on me, pulled me down, and I didn't yet feel as connected to anyone else. I could barely get myself to go past her room and I wouldn't visit her roommate. At the same time, I recognized that I had made a commitment, and that it didn't really matter how I felt about it. I had a working dog and she had a job to do. We showed up, we visited, Bella connected and comforted people in her wonderful dog ways, and every visit, every resident, was different.

Two things helped me. Helped a little. There was a cemetery near my home that was beautiful. It was really a park and had grave stones dating back to the 1700s. Bella loved going there as she could be off-leash and run. So on a cool June day, she and I were taking a walk there, which meant I was throwing a tennis ball and she was flying after it and bringing it back to me. I found it peaceful and was strolling along, humming to myself, when I saw a fresh grave. I walked over to it and bent down to read the head-stone: Beverly. And her last name and dates.

"Oh, my God," I said. "Beverly. It's Beverly. My Beverly."

Fighting back my tears, I told her how glad I was to know where she was. That I missed her. That I loved her.

Bella nudged my leg and looked longingly at the ball.

"I'm coming, girlfriend. I'm coming. Just give me a minute." And I stood there on a perfect, early summer day, and thought about her grin. Her wide-open crazy smile, her bruised hands, and her dolls. That bond was unbroken.

The other thing that helped me was a patient we met on one of our visits to the hospital with Deb and Shelby. We saw a woman about our age standing beside a patient's bed, and learned that the patient was her daughter, Katie. We saw right away that Katie had special needs and it looked to me as though she was in pain.

Her mother's face lit up when she saw the dogs. "Please bring them in. Katie loves dogs."

Katie was curled up in the bed, but when she saw Bella and Shelby, she uncurled and her face opened. I asked her if Bella could put her paws on the edge of the bed and she nodded. A smile appeared. Shelby got close enough that she could reach her, too. She touched both dogs and as she did, it looked as if her pain was gone. She was beaming.

"She used to have a lab," her mother told us. "She's crazy about dogs. You have no idea—"

She couldn't keep talking. I looked over at Deb and saw tears in her eyes. I knew she was thinking about Wendy.

We stayed, we were never in a hurry, but just as it was time to leave, Katie's mother turned to us and said, "It's been so long since I've seen Katie smile, I thought maybe I never would again. Today was a huge gift."

We told Katie that we really enjoyed meeting her and said good-bye to her and her mother. Out in the hallway, Deb and I didn't say a word to each other. We had tears in our eyes and we knew. We knew we had dogs who touched people's hearts, and this helped me see that Bella and I would continue this work without Beverly, and it would still be special.

🐾 🐾

But it wasn't easy. When a new resident appeared with the same first name, I couldn't say it out loud. There was only one. Her room was still her room. But over time, I noticed I couldn't prevent bonding. Alice and I had a funny language together. I said something and she said it back. We looked into each other's eyes, and sometimes I could pull her out of where she seemed to be stuck.

I said, "You look pretty," and she said, "Pretty." Then I said, "How's your pussy cat?" referring to the stuffed cat in her lap. No response. But if I said, "Meow," then she almost always meowed back. And after I blew her a kiss when we were leaving, her hand came up to her mouth and she did the best she could to send one back to me.

Ann was another one because she had a great attitude. She looked out the window in her room at two bird feeders and admired the birds, the motion, the signs of spring. She didn't complain. She said she had a tumor on her leg the size of a watermelon. I asked if it hurt and she said no, but I wondered. She loved Bella to get up on her bed and then she closed her hand over the treat and made Bella sniff and lick her hand before she gave it to her.

Joyce was yet another. She always had a book in her hand—her good hand. I didn't even see her other hand, the one bent into itself by a stroke, until I'd known her a year. She wore scarves and had a small cork board hung on her wall for all her earrings. Deb and I loved the stuffed monkey who resided on her bed until Joyce was too ill to get out of bed. The last time I saw her, I wasn't sure if she knew Bella and I were there. I told her that we loved getting to know her and that we would remember her.

As Deb and the two dogs and I made our way down the long hallways of the rehab facility, there were ghosts, shadows of the previous residents. I'd say to Deb, "Someone's in Frank's room," knowing she'd remember him. Or she'd say to me, "I miss Chuck," and we'd smile, thinking of the time he ate the dog treat. We loved his wife as much as him—she was so patient, so grateful for our visits.

I realized now that the joy Bella and Shelby brought took place where lives were broken. Where loss and sadness resided. But the dogs taught me that we were all in this together, and that what looked like a depressing place from the outside could be transformed by friendship and what we learned from each other. The residents all taught me something different: Olive, how to face death without a struggle. Karen, how stories last and can be passed on. Chuck, that the dogs we love stay beside us always. Betty, that having two dogs show up to celebrate your ninety-fifth birthday is better than cake. And Wendy, that love can be perfect even from a broken body. And Beverly, my wonderful Beverly, that you never know when someone will come along and be the mother you lost.

Like a dog unleashed running full out, like the white streak that was Bella, hunkered down, flying across a field, like Beverly's smile, like Deb's face when she said to a new resident "Would you like to see the dogs?"—like all that, joy breaks out. It fills the room, it's dappled light reflecting up from itself, up walls, up everything. It's what my father used to call "hiddy-haddies" for light shimmering on tree trunks at the edge of the water. There was no real way to capture it. None at all. But Bella didn't mind not having the words. She spoke fluently with her whole body, a gift to all she serves, and was simply joy unleashed.

A NOTE FROM THE AUTHOR

I was away during Beverly's funeral so had no way to say good-bye. No way to believe that she was really gone. I asked the head of volunteers if I could write a note to Beverly's family. She said yes. Here it is:

My dog, Bella, and I have been visiting Beverly almost every week for two years. Bella is a therapy dog, and we come to The Starfish Home on Wednesday afternoons. I wanted to leave you this note, as Beverly and I had become friends and I thought you'd like to know about our visits.

I started at Starfish in the spring of 2012 and Bella had only recently been certified, which means we didn't have much experience. But I was lucky enough to team up with Deb and Shelby, as they had been visiting Starfish for several months and were skilled at asking residents if they wanted to see a therapy dog. They knew how to comfort, heal, and make friends. Bella and I tagged along and learned from both of them.

When I first met Beverly, she was sitting on the edge of her bed holding a doll. She had a look on her face that scared me—hard to describe but she appeared angry. I quickly left the room and focused on other residents. But during the week before our next visit, I thought about her and wondered if there was some way I could get through to her. I didn't have any idea if she would be interested in my dog, Bella, or a visit from a stranger.

The following week, I sat on the bed next to her and told her my name, showed her how Bella loved to eat dog treats, and patted her baby—the doll she was holding. After several months of this, I sang a lullaby to the doll and Beverly smiled. It was a breakthrough. At first the staff didn't believe that she would almost always either smile or laugh when we were together, but once they saw it they recognized the bond that had grown between us. They saw we were friends.

And while she couldn't talk, her eyes were expressive and she often held my hand or fingered the edge of my sleeve. Sometimes she took hold of the badge I wore (this was Bella's therapy dog certification) and I told her what it was. Once or twice, on nice days, I took her outside (always with the nurses' permission) so that she could get a breath of fresh air.

My friend Deb often said, "Beverly loves you," and the feeling was, and still is, mutual. I will miss her. If there are any ways Bella and I can be of help, please let us know. Best, Jean

April 2014

FURTHER READING

Here's a list of books that I've found helpful, plus a few websites that give you additional information about therapy dog certification.

Rescuing Riley, Saving Myself: A Man and his Dog's Struggle to find Salvation, Zachary Anderegg with Pete Nelson, Skyhorse Publishing, 2013. While not about a therapy dog, this is an amazing story about the healing bond between a man suffering from PTSD and the dog he saves from the bottom of a canyon. A wonderful read.

A Dog Walks into a Nursing Home: Lessons in the Good Life from an Unlikely Teacher, Sue Halpern, Riverhead Hardcover, 2013. Halpern takes us inside a nursing home with her therapy dog, Pransky. While she reveals the power dogs have to comfort and make a difference, her approach is more philosophical and abstract. What I liked about this book is how Halpern's volunteer work with her dog filled a void after her daughter left for college and she became an empty nester.

The Possibility Dogs, Susannah Charleson, Houghton Mifflin Harcourt, 2014. This is an amazing book written by an author who tells her own personal story of working with her search and rescue dog, Puzzle. Like veterans suffering from traumatic stress, she struggles with deep anxiety issues brought on by this difficult work. Her gift is recognizing dogs who make good service or therapy dogs and training them for people who desperately need them.

Healing Companions: Ordinary Dogs and Their Extraordinary Power to Transform Lives, Jane Miller, New Page Books, 2009. Written by a therapist, this book focuses on the role of psychiatric service dogs and how dogs can help heal emotional issues. And while a therapy dog does not have this level of training, there are some strong similarities. Written for the lay person who may be training his or her own dog, this book demonstrates the amazing power dogs have to heal.

Therapy Dogs: Training Your Dog to Reach Others, Kathy Diamond Davis, Dogwise Publishing, 2002 (reprint of 1982 version). This book offers a good overview of the training process and includes an excellent bibliography.

To the Rescue: Found Dogs with a Mission, Elise Lufkin & Diana Walker, Skyhorse Publishing, 2009. While not a book about therapy dogs, this beautiful collection of photographs includes dogs, that like Bella were thrown away, and were given another chance. There is something special about these dogs who almost didn't make it.

Angel on a Leash: Therapy Dogs and the Lives They Touch, David Frei (the voice of the Westminster Kennel Club and founder of Angel on a Leash), BowTie Press, 2011. This book does a good job of demonstrating the power dogs have to heal. His foundation,

Angel on a Leash, has done a great deal to enhance the role of therapy dogs.

Paws and Effect: The Healing Power of Dogs, Sharon Sakson, Spiegel & Grau, 2007, 2009. Finely written, this book starts with ancient history—how dogs and people teamed up and then provides specific examples of individuals who become involved in training service dogs. There are moving stories about organizations that have been created to promote this work, such as one that provides free dog food to low income and homeless pet owners. The focus of this book is service dogs—a very different population than therapy dogs—and one that requires much more training and more demanding certifications.

A Dog Who's Always Welcome: Assistance and Therapy Dog Trainers Teach You How to Socialize and Train Your Companion Dog, Lorie Long, Howell Book House/Wiley, 2008. This is basically a training book but has some helpful pages on what makes a good therapy dog, the key things they must learn, and guidance for the handler or human partner.

The Power of Wagging Tails: A Doctor's Guide to Dog Therapy and Healing, Dawn Marcus, MD, demosHealth, 2011. This is an inspiring book that gives, from a physician's perspective, a look at the healing power of dogs. True stories are interspersed with research and studies, and Dr. Marcus uses her own two therapy dogs at work so she has firsthand experience of the powerful ways dogs affect us.

Therapy Dogs Today: Their Gifts, Our Obligation, Kris Butler, Funpuddle Publishing Associates, 2004. Written for both the therapy dog owners as well as healthcare professionals, this book gives a thorough overview of what therapy dogs accomplish and how best to manage their work in a wide range of institutions. The author focuses on the ethical use of therapy dogs and asks handlers to watch carefully to see if their dogs show signs of discomfort or stress.

Every Dog Has a Gift: true stories of dogs who bring hope and healing into our lives, Rachael McPherson, Tarcher/Penguin, 2010. This author is founder of The Good Dog Foundation—an organization dedicated to the use and certification of therapy dogs. Reading this book, and learning about her foundation, I realized that Bella would never have passed her test as it's much more rigorous than many other certifications. She does a nice job of showing the healing power of therapy dogs, but unlike my book, her examples are short—vignettes—and don't allow the reader to get to know either the therapy dog or the person they're visiting in-depth. She and her organization have also been instrumental in changing laws that prohibited dogs from working in hospitals.

Little Boy Blue: A Puppy's Rescue from Death Row and His Owner's Journey for Truth, Kim Kavin, Barron's Educational Series, 2012. This book is like a detective story as Kim investigates where her rescue dog came from, and what happened to him before she adopted him. It's a wonderful read and an important message for those who want to save dogs.

The Rescue at Dead Dog Beach: One Man's Quest to Find a Home for the World's Forgotten Animals, Steven McGarva, Dey Street Books, 2014. I refer to this book in my book, and it was really hard to read. But Steve didn't give up on the dogs he found at Dead Dog Beach, where Bella was also either born or dumped, and he has become a wonderful advocate for saving these dogs and preventing the cruelty that gives this beach in Puerto Rico its name.

THERAPY DOG WEBSITES/ ORGANIZATIONS

The Bright and Beautiful Therapy Dogs, Inc., www.golden-dogs.org. This is the organization in Pennsylvania that certified Bella in 2011.

Pet Partners, www.petpartners.org. According to their website, "Pet Partners is the national leader in demonstrating and promoting animal-assisted therapy, activities and education. Nearly forty years since the organization's inception, the science that proves these benefits has become indisputable. Today, Pet Partners is the nation's largest and most prestigious nonprofit registering handlers of multiple species as volunteer teams providing animal-assisted interventions."

The Good Dog Foundation, www.thegooddogfoundation.org. According to their website, "Good Dog is proud to provide certified therapy dog teams to over 350 partner facilities in NY, NJ, CT, and MA free of charge. Good Dog is the only certifying organization in NYC, and it boasts the largest resources of any certifying organization on the East coast. The Good Dog Difference promises a meaningful experience for both volunteers and those receiving Good Dog services." (See the book, *Every Dog Has a Gift*, listed above.)

Therapy Dogs International, www.tdi-dog.org. "Previously Therapy Dogs International, TDI® is a volunteer organization dedicated to regulating, testing and registration of therapy dogs and their volunteer handlers for the purpose of visiting nursing homes, hospitals, other institutions and wherever else therapy dogs are needed."

American Kennel Club Therapy Dog Program. See details at www.akc.org/events/title-recognition-program/therapy/

ACKNOWLEDGMENTS

There are so many to thank—so many who helped Bella and the making of this book. First, I'd like to thank Mary Eldergill of Amigos de los Animales PR, who found Bella and her siblings on Dead Dog Beach and fostered them until they were ready for the shelter and the long trip to Newark, New Jersey. The whole team at Amigos does so much for animals who need our help—a shout-out to Adri Galler Lastra, president and shelter director. And thanks to St. Hubert's Animal Welfare Center in North Branch, New Jersey, who took care of Bella until we adopted her at about four months old.

There are too many trainers and friends and other dogs who have all been part of Bella's upbringing to mention. You know who you are and I thank you. Lastly, I'm indebted to my wonderful editor, Nicole Frail, at Skyhorse Publishing. She's been great to work with and has made the book much stronger. And a big thanks to the whole team at Skyhorse.